HOLYHABITS
IN MESSY CHURCH

The Bible Reading Fellowship
15 The Chambers, Vineyard
Abingdon OX14 3FE
brf.org.uk

The Bible Reading Fellowship (BRF) is a Registered Charity (233280)

ISBN 978 0 85746 923 6
First published 2020
10 9 8 7 6 5 4 3 2 1 0
All rights reserved

Acknowledgements
Unless otherwise stated, scripture quotations are taken from The New Revised Standard Version of the Bible, Anglicised edition, copyright © 1989, 1995 by the Division of Christian Education of the National Council of the Churches of Christ in the United States of America. Used by permission. All rights reserved.

Scripture quotations marked NIV are taken from The Holy Bible, New International Version (Anglicised edition) copyright © 1979, 1984, 2011 by Biblica. Used by permission of Hodder & Stoughton Publishers, a Hachette UK company. All rights reserved. 'NIV' is a registered trademark of Biblica. UK trademark number 1448790.

Every effort has been made to trace and contact copyright owners for material used in this resource. We apologise for any inadvertent omissions or errors, and would ask those concerned to contact us so that full acknowledgement can be made in the future.

A catalogue record for this book is available from the British Library

Printed and bound in the UK by Zenith Media NP4 0DQ

HOLY**HABITS**
IN **MESSY CHURCH**

DISCIPLESHIP SESSIONS FOR CHURCHES

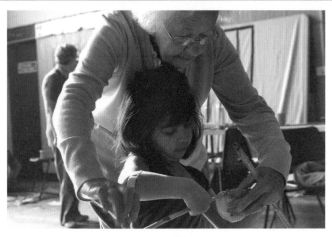

LUCY MOORE and **ANDREW ROBERTS**

Acknowledgements

With thanks to Jane Leadbetter and Ellie Bloxham for doggedly making so many weird objects and taking photos.

For Judith and Katie Moore, who bring so much creativity, diversity, surprise, challenge and love to our lives. And SO much mess.

Contents

Introduction

Andrew Roberts

Holy mess? Messy habits? The possibilities are many and, amid the fun, there is a recognition that Holy Habits and Messy Church are approaches to forming disciples of Jesus in ways that are both godly and down to earth. They experience holiness in hands covered in glue and paint. They are incarnational approaches (to use a theological word), continuing the Jesus tradition of seeking to be fully human in a divine way and striving for the kingdom to come on earth as it is in heaven. Crucially, they are both for ALL ages. In particular, they share a commitment to nurturing children, not as prototype disciples, not as people who will one day know enough to be called disciples, but who almost from the womb can be followers – and nurtured as followers – of Jesus.

They are both supportive of and anchored in the local church, whatever form that church takes. Both see gathering together and nurturing discipleship at home as important. Both encourage people to live out their faith day by day. They are ways of life.

Both Holy Habits and Messy Church emerge from a sense of gift. Neither are anybody's possession. They are gifts that God has given – that God is giving – to be opened and enjoyed and explored and shared. They're both shaped by everybody: one of the lovely gifts about both is that lots and lots of people of many different ages, cultures, nationalities and languages are contributing to the growth of both movements. There are no secret committees in concrete bunkers beneath big buildings masterminding schemes for how this shall all develop.

One of the gifts I still love to receive is Lego. We all know what people do with Lego kits: they empty out the pieces and look at the instruction booklet. They might follow the booklet once, but then they throw it away and begin to create all sorts of other wonderful things. That's precisely the spirit of both Messy Church and Holy Habits. Yes, there are guidelines and, yes, there is a certain amount of received wisdom about what might work well. But with both there is also a strong encouragement to be creative, imaginative and contextual.

Holy Habits is a way of life based upon Luke's model of the early church that we read of in Acts 2:42–47, a model that the biblical commentator C.K. Barrett argues is deliberately offered 'in order that we might imitate it' (*Acts 1—14*, T&T Clark, 2004, p. 160).

> They devoted themselves to the apostles' teaching and fellowship, to the breaking of bread and the prayers. Awe came upon everyone, because many wonders and signs were being done by the apostles. All who believed were together and had all things in common; they would sell their possessions and goods and distribute the proceeds to all, as any had need. Day by day, as they spent much time together in the temple, they broke bread at home and ate their food with glad and generous hearts, praising God and having the goodwill of all the people. And day by day the Lord added to their number those who were being saved.
>
> ACTS 2:42–47

In this picture, we see ten practices, or holy habits, that were hallmarks of the earliest Christian communities: biblical teaching, fellowship, breaking bread, prayer, sharing resources, serving, eating together, gladness and generosity, worship and making more disciples. According to Professor James Dunn, these hallmarks are present whenever we see 'enthusiastic spiritual renewal' (*The Acts of the Apostles*, Epworth, 1996, p. 34). They are certainly encouraged and happily often seen in Messy Churches.

In the text, Luke gives us some clues as to how these habits can be lived fruitfully. It's interesting to note how these clues are also keys to the fruitfulness of Messy Churches. He begins by saying 'they devoted themselves', and, unsurprisingly, both Holy Habits and Messy Church are proving to be fruitful when there is a high level of commitment to making disciples and living out this way of life.

Luke repeatedly uses the word 'all', and again we see fruit whenever as many people as possible – of all ages – are encouraged to be involved. (The Holy Habits resource booklets were first developed by a large number of people of all ages and backgrounds in the Birmingham Methodist Circuit, including ecumenical partners. The booklets published by BRF have even more contributors from even more traditions – around 200 people in total, including several children.)

Twice Luke uses the phrase 'day by day', reminding us that discipleship is for living in the whole of life. He notes that the Acts 2 community enjoyed 'the goodwill of all the people', challenging us to think how we can practise holy habits and be church in ways that bless the wider community.

And in the final verse, Luke says, 'The Lord added to their number', reminding us that this is God's work. With the passage located in the wake of the events of Pentecost, we are reminded that the life-giving breath of the Spirit is vital if we are to see growth and renewal, blessing and transformation.

Holy Habits is a way of life that we experience and practise to honour God and bless others, and it is to be lived day by day. As such, it is naturally evangelistic. Now there is a word that makes some nervous, but it literally means 'good news', so we should not be surprised if the Lord adds to the number of people who become disciples of Jesus when the Acts 2 picture is lived out in our times. After all, who would not want to be part of a community that is glad and generous, eats together, gives to any as they have need, serves, prays and has vibrant worship? That looks like Messy Church at its best.

Holy Habits is also a sacramental way of life: sacramental in the specific sense of the word, encouraging as it does the practices of baptism and Holy Communion. It is sacramental, too, in the more general sense of the word, living a life of embodied grace to be a sign of the kingdom.

I began by playing with the words 'holy and 'messy'. Commenting on the call of Jesus to make disciples (Matthew 28:19), Sean Stillman of Zac's Place in Swansea says, 'Building disciples is an unbelievably messy process and I think it was messy for Jesus and it continues to be so for us' (Norman Ivison, *Expressions: Making a difference*, Fresh Expressions, 2011, chapter 28). Sometimes in Messy Church, the mess will be the creative mess of glue, paint and junk modelling. Sometimes it will be the messiness of our lives or the lives of those we are called to serve. Sometimes we can be nervous of the word 'holy', because we think it speaks of an impossible perfection we can never attain. I increasingly think the struggle to be holy is the struggle to be fully human in a Christlike way. And that's one reason why God has gifted us one another in Messy Churches: to explore and practise holy habits when we gather together – and to encourage and support one another as we seek to live out this messy, holy way of life in the mission fields of our day-to-day lives.

For more on Holy Habits, go to holyhabits.org.uk.

Holy Habits by Andrew Roberts (Malcolm Down Publishing, 2017) is an in-depth exploration of the biblical background to Holy Habits, packed full of stories of everyday people living out this way of life.

Introduction

Lucy Moore

Messy Church is helping people of all ages enjoy being on a journey with Jesus together. Whether people arrive at church full of excitement about him or are only interested in what's for tea, Jesus welcomes us just as we are and longs for every person, young and old, seasoned church member and I'm-just-looking visitor, to walk closer to him. This book, based on ten habits of the early Jesus-followers from the period soon after Jesus' resurrection, as described in Acts 2:42–47, is one approach to Messy discipleship. It builds the idea of developing our beliefs, behaviours and attitudes into the very themes of eleven Messy Church sessions. In other words, one way of making and growing disciples in Messy Church is to use this material in your sessions. If you need to enrich the ideas offered here, the *Get Messy!* magazine sessions between May 2019 and April 2020 also feature the Holy Habits, using different Bible passages. (These are available to purchase from brfonline.org. uk/collections/get-messy.)

If you're new to Messy Church, do check out this exciting movement of God by reading all about it at messychurch.org.uk and in the Messy Church books before you launch in and use the sessions in this book. Many people think they know what Messy Church is, only to discover there's more to it than meets the eye. (Or indeed, ear, stomach or nose. Multisensory is our middle name.)

As befits Messy Church, some of the activities in this book are completely barking mad, and that's all part of the fun. When we get too solemn, it's time to close down. After all, **celebration** is one of our five values. What of the other values? **Creativity** continues to be key and, even if you only take part in half the activities in the book, you'll be stretching your imaginative muscles nicely. **Hospitality** means that, once again, we are setting out to be the most generous hosts and most humble guests we can be, expecting to learn about these habits from the very youngest and very oldest participants. Messy Church's attraction lies partly in the way we are **all ages together** – we are deliberately and intentionally intergenerational, as we believe it's the best way of growing as disciples for a long-term faith. So as we go through these sessions, let's keep looking for what God is teaching us through those who are mightily different from us. And at the heart of everything is **Christ**, making our Messy Churches so much more than just a fun family time with food. Christ is walking among us, sitting beside us, laughing with us and listening to us. He is weeping, challenging, guiding, bracing and helping us become the holy priesthood he wants his whole church to become. As I was pulling together the material for this book, I kept realising afresh how the whole church needs to develop its understanding of these spiritual practices, not just Messy Churches.

Many churches are already using the Holy Habits approach in mainstream church life. You can read more about it at holyhabits.org.uk. In fact, during the writing of this book, we've had several requests for sessions to help Messy Churches match their theme to that of the Holy Habits happening in their Sunday church. Thank you to those churches who have trialled the sessions as a result.

A word about the selection of Bible passages. We've deliberately focused each session on a gospel passage about Jesus, to make the sessions as Christ-centred as possible and to give us every excuse for discovering what a wonderful God he is. This includes the first session, which although it explores the key passage in Acts 2 on which Holy Habits is based, in order to give a context to the habits as a whole, has a gospel theme of following Jesus the good shepherd. You might get to the end of the year and find yourself desperate to revisit the Old Testament.

So what have we provided here for each Holy Habit?

For each Holy Habit (Gladness and Generosity, Making More Disciples, Sharing Resources, Serving, Biblical Teaching , Eating Together, Worship, Prayer, Breaking Bread, Fellowship), you'll find a typical Messy Church layout, with guidance for the team to read so everyone can get their bearings with the passage. There are suggestions for making the most of the opportunities Messy Church gives for helping people grow in Christ together (ideas to get the team thinking, questions for the meal tables, ideas to take home). There are ten activities on the habit, a celebration suggestion and a meal suggestion. Photos and videos of most of the activities can be found at messychurch.org.uk/holyhabitsinmessychurch for that 'Oh, I see!' experience after being baffled by the printed instructions.

At the end of each session is a Messy Extra outline. Some churches are now holding Messy Extra groups for families who want to explore the things of faith further. So each Holy Habit has a very simple, robust outline for such a group to use with all ages present. You'll find a Bible passage that relates to the Holy Habit theme, with some discussion questions to use in your all-age setting. As Johannah Myers' research in the USA demonstrated, children especially appreciate *doing* more than just *talking*, so a fun themed activity suggestion for the group is provided, suitable to do in a smaller group than a Messy Church. Don't be tempted to miss this out, as it represents the celebratory, relational, light-hearted and participatory side of Messy Church, and perhaps some of the adults will benefit from loosening up a bit and learning once more how to play – a valuable aspect of our discipleship. There's also a prayer idea to use in such a Messy Extra group.

The Messy Extras are all explorations of the ways the early Jesus-followers practised these habits, as described in Acts and in the epistles to the Corinthians. These Extras have dictated the order in which we've placed the sessions in this book, as they follow the order they appear in the Bible. If you're just using the Messy Church sessions, you can, of course, do the sessions in any order.

Lastly, if you run a Messy Vintage group (see messychurch.org.uk/messyvintage), there is a separate, shorter outline which includes just one of the main session activities and a simplified celebration, suitable for where the majority of people are older or space is more limited.

You could match your Messy Church sessions to the Holy Habits programme used by the rest of your church. You could intersperse these Holy Habits sessions with the 2019–20 *Get Messy!* magazine sessions, spending two months on each habit, making a note of which magazine sessions you leave aside so you can use them later. You could use the sessions as one-offs at special times of the year (for example, Prayer during Pentecost; Eating Together at Harvest; Breaking Bread just before Easter). You could have a weekend away and indulge in all the sessions in a very concentrated way. Or simply explore one a month for the best part of a year.

We'd love to hear of any lives transformed by God as you use these materials, or supplementary ideas you have that we can share more widely in our networks in the UK and overseas. Feel free to drop us a line at messychurch@brf.org.uk.

I really wish we could have found a way of introducing a football activity into one of the sessions, but it wasn't possible. I just wanted to call one activity 'Kicking the habit'. Perhaps you'll find a way...

Photos of activities and other PDF downloads for these activities can be found at **messychurch.org.uk/holyhabitsinmessychurch**.

1

The Jesus habit

> [Jesus said,] 'I am the good shepherd. The good shepherd lays down his life for the sheep. The hired hand, who is not the shepherd and does not own the sheep, sees the wolf coming and leaves the sheep and runs away – and the wolf snatches them and scatters them. The hired hand runs away because a hired hand does not care for the sheep. I am the good shepherd. I know my own and my own know me, just as the Father knows me and I know the Father. And I lay down my life for the sheep. I have other sheep that do not belong to this fold. I must bring them also, and they will listen to my voice. So there will be one flock, one shepherd.'
>
> JOHN 10:11–16

#discipleship

Messy team theme

- How do you feel about exploring these holy habits?
- Which habit are you most looking forward to exploring?
- Which habit do you think will be most challenging?

How does this session help people grow in Christ?

This session can be left out completely if you simply want to explore the ten holy habits. But we include it as an overview of the whole idea that being a follower of Jesus means living differently – in fact, it means forming new habits and breaking away from old unhelpful ones. The image Jesus uses of sheep following a trustworthy shepherd might be helpful to people who have never thought about 'discipleship' before. So this session simply introduces the concept of following Jesus, a bit like sheep following a shepherd.

Mealtime card

- What's the worst habit someone could have?
- What's the funniest habit you've ever heard of?
- What are you most looking forward to about practising a holy habit?

Take-home idea

Take home a packet of copper sulphate. At home, dissolve the copper sulphate in a glass of water and hang a thread into it. Watch over the weeks as crystals form on the thread. Talk about the slow way this happens and the way we all practise holy habits to become slowly more and more like Jesus.

Question to start and end the session

So… what is following Jesus all about?

Activities

1 Sheep on a stick

You will need: halved bananas; melted white chocolate; melted dark chocolate; white and dark chocolate buttons or chocolate chips; long wooden skewers; greaseproof paper

Stick your chunk of banana on a skewer and dip it in the white chocolate. You might be able to make a textured coat by twirling the banana as the chocolate sets or by putting patterns into it using a second kebab skewer. Dip the tip into the dark chocolate to make a dark face. Stick on two eyes made from chocolate buttons and/or chips. Allow to set completely on the greaseproof paper.

Talk about how Jesus wants us to follow him and trust him, like sheep follow and trust a shepherd. What do you think that means in our lives?

2 Transfer

You will need: wide sticky tape; scissors; magazine pictures (perhaps of sheep, if you want to stick with the theme, but they could be of anything); a shallow dish of water

Cut a piece of sticky tape and stick it over your chosen picture. Cut out the shape of the transfer you want, with the picture or pattern within that shape. Put the shape in the water and go away for five minutes (resist the urge to piggle at it before five minutes are up or you'll damage your picture). Gently, with your thumbnail, scrape away the paper pulp behind your picture, leaving the picture on the tape. Allow it to dry, then you can take it home and stick it to your window, plastic box, filing cabinet or any other shiny surface.

Talk about how when we follow Jesus, we try to become more and more like him. This transfer is a copy of the original picture, now in a new form. We're meant to be ourselves not 'exact copies of Jesus', but we want to copy the way he lives and deals with other people. If more people became more like Jesus, what do you think the world would be like?

3 String bowl

You will need: cling film; small cardboard bowls; PVA glue; paint brushes; thick string

Cover the bowl in two or three layers of cling film. Paint glue thickly all over the outside of the bowl. With the bowl upside down and starting in the centre of the base, coil around 50 cm of string into a tight spiral glued on to the base of the bowl. Then keep winding string around the bowl from there with lots of glue until you almost reach the rim. Cover it with more glue. Take home to dry for several days (hence using a cardboard bowl, not a church bowl that may never be seen again). When it's properly dry, gently peel off the clingfilm and release the stiff string bowl.

Talk about the way your new bowl is moulded on an older bowl. Who or what do you want to mould your habits in life? Social media? YouTube? People you'll never know? Or Jesus, the 'good shepherd'?

4 Mirror game

You will need: two chairs

Place the two chairs facing each other and invite two people to sit on them. Name them A and B. A starts by making some simple slow hand movements. B imagines that they are A's reflection in a mirror and tries to copy as exactly and in perfect synchronicity as they can. Swap over after a short time. Then let them confer secretly and decide who will lead and who will follow. Challenge any people watching to guess whether A or B is the 'leader' as they do some more actions.

Talk about the fact that it's very hard and takes a lot of concentration to follow the leader in every exact detail. How hard is it to follow Jesus, would you say? What does it mean to follow Jesus anyway?

5 Holy Habits pie

You will need: card; coloured pens; plates; rulers; a list of the ten holy habits or the names printed on stickers (more hassle but more fun)

On card, draw around the plate to make a circle and use the ruler to divide it up into ten sections. Label it 'Holy Habits pie' and label each pie slice with the name of a habit. Decorate it.

Talk about how you could take this home and keep it safe and try to colour in each slice as you explore them at Messy Church over the next year or so. (Make it clear it's not about colouring it all in at once, but as a marker that you've explored a particular habit.) You could offer a prize for anyone who brings it back filled in at the end of the year.

6 Holy Habits memory game

You will need: pairs of cards with the ten holy habits and symbols on (download online)

Play Pelmanism (the game where you put all the cards face down spread across a table and turn up two at a time, trying to find the matching pairs).

Talk about whether you can remember all ten holy habits.

7 Spot the habit

You will need: printouts of Acts 2:42–47; cards with a holy habit on each (download online)

Challenge people to find each habit in the passage: it's a description of what the first Jesus-followers did and how they followed Jesus in their everyday lives.

Talk about which habit you found most interesting? Do you think it's possible to have these habits today? Who do you know who has any of them already?

8 Who is this Jesus?

You will need: outline of a person on a large sheet of paper; pens

Around the outside of the outline, draw or write things you can remember that Jesus did (such as actions, miracles, healings, acts of kindness, cosmic achievements). On the inside, draw or write things that he was (adjectives, names, 'job descriptions').

Talk about why people have followed Jesus for 2,000 years – and still do.

9 Building blocks

You will need: any sort of construction materials, such as soaked dried peas and toothpicks, spaghetti and marshmallows, Lego bricks, toy bricks

Invite people to build as strong a building as they can: something that is resilient when shaken or pushed or when heavy loads are placed on it.

Talk about what makes a structure strong. What makes a person's life 'strong'? How might building holy habits into your life help you when you feel wobbly, under pressure or weighed down? How long does it take to build a resilient structure? How long does it take to develop a habit?

10 Treasure hunt

You will need: a selection of ten containers that resemble treasure chests as much as possible (though you could just use envelopes); cards that can fit into your containers; a prize (such as a suitable Bible or gospel or a Messy minibook – *Family Question Time, Family Prayer Time* **or** *Family Jesus Time***); pens**

Write the letters from H O L Y H A B I T S on separate cards and put one in each chest. Hide the chests around your space. Send people on a quest to find the letters that together make up two words that lead to a treasure. Give a prize to the quickest person.

Talk about what 'holy habits' we might mean. How can habits be good or bad? In what way could holy habits lead to any sort of treasure? What might this treasure be?

Celebration

(You might like to think in advance about the pastoral implications for this celebration for people with a destructive habit, such as a drug addiction.)

Talk about a bad habit you once had and have (perhaps!) managed to stop. Ask what a 'habit' is.

What bad habits can people think of? Why is it so hard to stop once you start?

But what if *good* habits were just as hard to stop once you start? What if you just couldn't help doing holy things once you catch the habit? Wouldn't that be great?

Here at Messy Church, over the next few months, we're going to explore ten 'holy habits' that people who follow Jesus have found helpful in getting to know Jesus better.

They're not about 'being good'; they're about getting as close as we can to Jesus, just like sheep want to be as close as they can be to the shepherd who looks after them.

So who can remember any of the holy habits we're going to discover together?

The first people to follow Jesus had much harder lives than we do. If they were caught worshipping Jesus, they could be thrown in prison – even killed (as some Christians are today in some countries). The first Jesus-followers needed to help each other be strong and keep on following Jesus, even when it was hard, even when it was dangerous. And do you know what made it easier? They were *together*. They helped each other. They knew they were never alone. *Together* they prayed, read God's word and worshipped God. *Together* they served their community and were generous to each other. They had meals together and broke bread together. They even shared their possessions with each other so nobody was in need.

I wonder how we can help each other catch these holy habits and follow our good shepherd even more closely? Perhaps just being *together* at Messy Church is a really good start. Has anyone got any other ideas?

Prayer

Have a large sheet of paper with 'I want to follow Jesus more closely' written on it. Invite everyone who would like to follow Jesus more closely to sign their name or draw a picture of themselves beneath the words. Thank God that you are all together on this adventure and ask God for help to follow Jesus more closely, like sheep following a wonderful shepherd.

Song suggestions

- 'We're on this road' – Fischy Music
- 'Celebrate' – Fischy Music
- 'The Lord's my shepherd' – Stuart Townend

Meal suggestion

Shepherd's pie

Messy Extra

Acts 2:42–47:
What did the first Jesus-followers do?

Read the passage together.

- What do you find most interesting?
- What word or phrase stands out for you?
- How is your church or group like this already?
- Is there anything you would be really excited about trying out yourselves?
- What difference will this story make this week in the way you choose to worship Jesus?

Activity

Using Lego or other construction equipment, and the internet for ideas and images, build the sort of first-century house that the early followers of Jesus in Corinth, Rome or similar cities might have met in. Does it give you any insights into how their meetings together might have felt?

Prayer

Use the construction materials again. Build a prayer sculpture by adding one piece at a time to a joint structure in the centre of the group with a prayer for someone in need, then somewhere that needs Jesus' light, then your local church, etc.

2

Gladness and Generosity

> Then the son said to him, 'Father, I have sinned against heaven and before you; I am no longer worthy to be called your son.' But the father said to his slaves, 'Quickly, bring out a robe – the best one – and put it on him; put a ring on his finger and sandals on his feet. And get the fatted calf and kill it, and let us eat and celebrate; for this son of mine was dead and is alive again; he was lost and is found!' And they began to celebrate.
>
> LUKE 15:21–24

#discipleship

Messy team theme

- What have you got too much of?
- When you see something overflowing, do you feel sad or glad?
- Do you run your Messy Church from a sense of plenty or a sense of poverty?

How does this session help people grow in Christ?

The early followers of Jesus 'ate their food with glad and generous hearts' (Acts 2:46). Generosity has nothing to do with material wealth: very poor people can be very generous and very wealthy people can be very miserly. Generosity is closely related to 'gladness' or a sense of gratitude and awareness of all we've been given – not what we don't have. This session helps us think about the generosity of God overflowing into generosity to others around us.

Mealtime card

- If you won a million pounds, how much would you keep?
- If you were given the gift of another whole day of being alive, how would you spend it? (Wait… isn't that what tomorrow is?)
- What's the best gift you've ever been given?

Take-home idea

Say a thank-you ping-pong prayer at bedtime. Take it in turns to say, 'Thank you God for…' 'And for…' 'And for…', and see who can keep going longest.

Question to start and end the session

So… why are Christians so generous?

Activities

1 Wallet

You will need: 1l fruit juice or milk tetrapacks, washed and dried; coloured tape (electrical tape is good); scissors; stick-on Velcro dots

This is MUCH easier to make than to explain in writing – don't be put off, give it a go!

Flatten the carton so the sides have gussets. Cut off the top and bottom of the carton. Cut the top 3 cm square out of both sides at one end and round off the corners of one of the flaps to be the folding flap.

Fold the carton in half doubled up on itself, up to the bottom of the 3 cm cut in the sides. Tuck the spare flap inside and fold over the rounded flap. Cover the raw edges with tape. Use Velcro dots to join together the two halves in the centre and to stick down the flap.

Talk about how the first followers of Jesus made sure all the church members shared what they had. Will your wallet be for keeping money in for yourself or for taking money out of to share with others?

2 Gumball generosity machine

You will need: lots of clean plastic bottles; scissors; coloured tape; paper cups; decorations for the cups (coloured pens, bling, stickers and so on); pom-poms; print-off of the gladness and generosity ideas (download online); glue

Decorate the paper cup base if desired. Then cut the shoulders off two identical bottles so that you have two halves of a globe. Cut the neck off one of these. Leave the cap screwed on to the other neck.

Cover the raw edges with tape. Tape over the hole left by the neck on one half. Tape the two halves together on one side to make a hinge. Tape the globe on to the paper cup base, with the screw top at the top.

Now choose seven gladness and generosity ideas, cut them out and stick them on to seven pom-poms. Put the pom-poms in the globe. Shake well.

Talk about whether you can you open up your machine and pick out one generosity idea to do every day this week.

3 God's generous heart

You will need: paper; a heart-shaped stencil (download online); wax crayons; paper; hard pencil or biro; paper clips

Use the wax crayons to colour all over a sheet of paper with lots of different colours so there's no white space showing. Tuck the coloured-in paper, coloured side down, into the fold of a piece of paper doubled over on itself, as a sort of sandwich. Paper clip the stencil shape on to the top paper. Use a hard pencil or biro to colour in the stencil's shaded areas.

Talk about the different ways that God is generous to you. How many ways can you count? How might we be more generous in Messy Church to show people how generous our God is?

4 Watering can

You will need: empty, clean, plastic milk bottles and lids; an awl or similar sharp tool; protective board for table; marker pens (optional)

Challenge everyone to design the best-pouring watering can. With the awl, make one small hole in the handle of the bottle and several small holes in the lid. Decorate the bottle with marker pens if desired. Fill the bottle with water and test its pouring ability. Make more holes or larger ones if required.

Talk about the way the son in the story poured away his father's money on having a good time and the way the father in the story poured out his money into a party for his son's return. Who was right? What do you think Jesus' listeners thought? What do you think? Is there a bad way to be generous?

5 Overflowing generosity

You will need: bottle of cola; tube of Mentos mints; an outdoor space; a paper funnel (optional)

Do we need to explain this famous activity? Take the lid off the bottle of cola and pour in a tube of Mentos in as swift a movement as you can, then run for cover.

Talk about the way the bottle bubbles over with liquid. Who do you know who bubbles over with generosity with their time, attention, hugs or love? Have you ever thought of God being like this experiment?

6 Bubble snakes

You will need: plastic bottles with the base cut off; old clean socks; elastic bands; dishes of soapy water

Stretch a sock over the open base of the bottle so that it's taut; fasten it in place with an elastic band if necessary. Dip the sock into the soapy water. Then blow – DON'T SUCK – into the neck of the bottle. Enjoy the foamy snake that comes out – how long can you make it? Experiment with different-density socks and socks with holes in them.

Talk about the way the breath fills the liquid as it filters through the sock and turns it into an extravagant sculpture, far bigger than you might have expected. Can you think of any Bible stories where you see Jesus being surprisingly generous? When has God's generosity surprised you? When has someone else's generosity surprised you?

7 Champagne fountain

You will need: at least 20 goblets or cups (unbreakable); jugs or bottles of water (or champagne if you have the budget); an outside space or a paddling pool to catch the liquid

Set the goblets or cups up in as high a pyramid as you can build. Pour the water or champagne into the top one and see how long it takes to fill all the goblets. Try different configurations. What works best? Why?

Talk about the way the water overflows from one goblet into the others as long as you keep pouring water into it. What do you think helps people be generous with what they have? Who might you describe as 'empty' in some way? How do we get 'filled up' to 'overflow' to people who are emptier than us?

8 Big drip art

You will need: a gantry, as large as you can make it (or a beam, branch of a tree or similar); big sheets of paper; liquid paint; string; a container with a hole in

Suspend the container by the string to the gantry so it hangs over the paper. Pour in some paint and set it swinging or circling. See what patterns you can make as the paint drips or pours on to the paper.

Talk about the way the container has to empty itself to make the artwork. The Bible talks about God pouring the Holy Spirit out on us through Jesus (Titus 3:5–6). How did Jesus pour himself out to people? How do you feel about God's generosity to you?

9 Fruit smoothie

You will need: fruit; milk (maybe dairy-free milk); fruit juices; blender; cups; knives; chopping boards (if the fruit needs chopping)

Invite people to design the best smoothie ever and make it. Make a big thing of pouring it out of the blender.

Talk about the way the human body can't have too much vitamin C (unless you go to really ridiculous lengths): the body just gets rid of what it doesn't need. You can never have too much! What else can you never have too much of? What does God want to pour out on you? What would you like to pour out into the world around you?

10 Freely felt-tipping

> **You will need: black pens; other colouring pens; paper; a copy of Matthew 10:8 ('Freely you have received; freely give', NIV); a Bible**

Turn Jesus' words in Matthew 10:8 into a colouring poster for someone else in your family to colour in. Make sure it has something in its design that you want that person to understand about what these words might mean for them (a picture of something they've received freely, for example).

Talk about whether you prefer to give or receive. What do you consider yourself to have received freely? Check out the Bible – who was Jesus talking to and what did he mean?

Celebration

> **You will need: plenty of pens; some small cardboard heart shapes (enough for everyone to have one)**

Tell the story of the prodigal son in your own words, with a focus particularly on the way the younger son poured out his father's money until he had none left, and the way the father poured out his jewellery, clothes and food on his son to celebrate his return.

Who was the silliest person in the story and why?

- Was it the younger son, because he wasted everything?
- Was it the father, because he wasted all those lovely things in giving a party?
- Or was it the older brother, who didn't want to waste anything at all?

The very first followers of Jesus decided they wanted to live their whole lives as close as they possibly could to how Jesus wanted them to be. One of the ways they lived was 'with glad and generous hearts'. What sort of a difference do you think it made to the people around them, that they had 'glad and generous hearts'?

Who do you know at work or school or home or here in church who has a glad and generous heart? (*You might want to tell the story of someone in your church who did something really generous recently. Or you could tell one of the stories from pp. 36–39 of the Gladness and Generosity Holy Habits booklet.*)

Give everybody a cardboard cut-out of a heart and invite them to draw a smiley face on it and put it in their pocket or handbag or sock to remind them to try to be as glad and generous as the father in the story today.

Prayer

Dear Jesus, as we put these heart shapes in a safe place, we ask for your help to make us glad and generous towards everyone we meet this week. Amen

Song suggestions

- 'God beside' – Fischy Music
- 'Holding on to the rock' – Fischy Music
- 'Amazing grace' – John Newton

Meal suggestion

Spaghetti bolognaise

Messy Extra

Acts 3:1–11: Peter heals a lame beggar

Read through the story together and, if you have the space to, act it out.

- What other stories does this remind you of?
- What's different about this one?
- What do you like best in this story?
- Is anybody 'glad' or 'generous' in this story? How?
- Is generosity always about money?
- What does this story mean for us today?

Activity

Carve potato stampers together. Play 'Minute to Win It', seeing who can stamp the highest number of stamps on a piece of paper, using your potatoes and an old sponge soaked in paint, within a minute. Use this to talk about the way the first followers of Jesus seemed to pour God's generous love out of them, like you trying to print as many shapes as you could: they never ran out of God's love.

Prayer

On heart shapes, draw or write somebody you want to feel God's gladness and generosity at the moment. Place them next to a cross or a lit candle.

3

Making More Disciples

> Now the eleven disciples went to Galilee, to the mountain to which Jesus had directed them. When they saw him, they worshipped him; but some doubted. And Jesus came and said to them, 'All authority in heaven and on earth has been given to me. Go therefore and make disciples of all nations, baptising them in the name of the Father and of the Son and of the Holy Spirit, and teaching them to obey everything that I have commanded you. And remember, I am with you always, to the end of the age.'
>
> MATTHEW 28:16–20

#discipleship

Messy team theme

- What are you most delighted about in your Messy ministry?
- How many nations are represented by your Messy Church families?
- Jesus said, 'Go', and not, 'Invite the nations to come to you': have you any thoughts about taking your Messy Church out to people who don't come?

How does this session help people grow in Christ?

It is so easy for any Christian group to become inward-looking. Jesus' challenge or commission to 'go' reminds us all to stay outward-facing and make sure our church is always welcoming to newcomers and always focused on those outside its walls whom Jesus wants as his disciples too. We should never keep him to ourselves!

Mealtime card

- What good news has someone shared with you recently?
- How do you like to see or hear the news? On your phone? On TV?
- Who was the first person to tell you anything about Jesus?

Take-home idea

Make a thank-you card and send it to someone who has shared the good news of Jesus with you.

Question to start and end the session

So… what are Jesus' disciples meant to do?

Activities

1 Lip balm

You will need: small jars or pots (or old well-washed lip balm containers); washi tape and stickers (optional); grated beeswax; coconut oil; peppermint oil; vitamin E capsules (optional); bright lipstick (optional); microwaveable jug; microwave

Check for allergies before doing this activity. Decorate the container if you want to, using washi tape or stickers. The basic ratio is one part beeswax (grated) to one part coconut oil. Melt the two together in the microwave without boiling it. Stir in a few drops of peppermint oil, a drop or two of vitamin E from the capsules (acts as a preservative) and a small chunk of lipstick, if desired, to colour it. Microwave again briefly if required. Mix up the ingredients and pour carefully into the containers. Place in the fridge to set.

Talk about how Jesus told his friends to 'make disciples'. Some of the ways we make more disciples involve our mouths, so every time we use our lip balm, we can let it remind us of what Jesus asks us to do. We might get the journey started by telling other people how amazing we think Jesus is, inviting them to join us at church, praying for them in words… What else can you think of?

2 Rolling-pin painting

You will need: rolling pins; paper; pieces of sponge; paint; cling film; paper towel; cardboard; foil

Drench the sponge pieces in paint and place them on the paper. Use the rolling pin to roll out the paint in different shapes. Does it make any difference if you place a sheet of clingfilm or the other materials over the sponge before you roll?

Talk about the way the paint spreads out from the sponge. Jesus asks his disciples to spread his kingdom by making more disciples who can join in the work of changing the world for the better. Who could you help find out about Jesus?

3 Spin the word out!

You will need: a salad spinner; paper cut into circles; watery paint

Fit a circle of paper into the spinner basket. Blob paint on top of the paper, then put the lid on and spin! Take the paper out and see what sort of patterns are made with different colour combinations.

Talk about how, just as the paint gets flung out from the centre by centrifugal force, Jesus told his disciples to take God's word out to the ends of the earth in their quest to make more disciples. How much 'force' would it take to help you share the good news of Jesus with someone? How might the Holy Spirit be a 'force' to help you?

4 Junk disciple

You will need: junk items; sticky tape; scissors

Using the junk, build a disciple who's really good at making more disciples. What's special about your disciple? What do they particularly need? (A mouth that works? Beautiful feet? Hard-working hands? Long arms?) Do we need more than one disciple to be the best possible disciple?

Talk about what disciples do as we follow Jesus to make more disciples. What are we already good at and what could we be better at?

5 Good news!

You will need: newspaper templates (download online); pens (or a laptop to fill in the news headlines electronically)

Give each person a sheet with the headline 'Best news about Jesus: _____!' and invite them to think what they believe is the best news about Jesus and to fill in the rest of the headline with words that will make people want to read the rest of the report. Draw the pictures in, too.

Talk about how, when we hear good news, we want other people to know it, too. What is the best news about Jesus that will really help your friends want to know him and follow him, too?

6 Fruity disciples

You will need: different-coloured fruit cut into slices, chunks or pieces; plates; honey; toothpicks; raisins; poppy seeds

Portion out equal amounts of a variety of fruit pieces on to plates. The challenge is to make as many disciples as you can out of your allocation of pieces of fruit. You can 'glue' details on using raisins, seeds and honey, using the toothpicks as spreaders. Look at the variety of different-looking 'disciples' you've made!

Talk about how Jesus asks his disciples to make more disciples. I don't think he meant to do it out of fruit: what do you think he meant? Have you ever made a (non-fruity) disciple?

7 Throw 'n' pray

You will need: the template of a cube (download online); coloured pens; scissors; sticky tape

Draw or write the names of five friends you'd like to introduce to Jesus, one on each face of the cube. Put yourself on the final face. Cut it out, fold it and stick it together to make a die. Decide on a time each day to roll the die and pray for the person who is on the uppermost face.

Talk about the fact that, when we decide to make more disciples, we're not alone. The Holy Spirit is our helper and gives us a helping hand. The best way we can ask for help is by praying.

8 Disco ball

You will need: thread; polystyrene balls (from craft suppliers); either sequins and pins, small self-adhesive mirror mosaic squares or holographic wrapping paper cut into small squares; glue; a light source

Attach thread to the polystyrene ball so it will hang like a Christmas tree ornament. Then completely cover the surface with your reflective pieces: either pin on the sequins or stick on the other materials. Hang it up and shine a light on it to see the light reflecting off it.

Talk about the way the light shines from the source and bounces off the dazzling disco ball, sending light into all sorts of directions. When our lives reflect the light of Jesus, we will find his love is sent out from us into all sorts of dark places, making more disciples on the way.

9 Invitation

You will need: cards; fun things to decorate them with

Ask people to think of one person they could invite to the part of church they enjoy most (e.g. Messy Church, Sunday church, home group) and then to make an invitation for that person and their family to give to them before next time. What would they enjoy most about it? Make sure that's clear on your design, alongside the date/time/place.

Talk about how Jesus asked his friends to make more disciples: we can do it, too. Inviting someone along to the part of church we enjoy most is a good start.

10 Make disciples of all nations

You will need: pieces of card saying 'good news about Jesus'; signs for ten different countries that have significance for your church; a spinner with the same countries on; a timer

Place the country signs on ten different chairs or scattered around your space. Put the cards in a pile next to the competitor. Start the timer and spin the spinner.

Whichever country the arrow lands on, this is the country the competitor should run to, taking a card with the good news on and leaving it on the country's chair before running back to spin again and repeating for a different country. See how many countries the competitor can take the good news cards to within a minute. (If you don't have room to run around, do a similar version but as a table-top game, simply placing the card on the right country's name on a table top.)

Talk about people who have been brave enough to take the good news of Jesus to other countries. Perhaps your church supports a missionary family or has a connection with a particular country: tell the story of how faith came to that country.

Celebration

(This celebration echoes a page in the Messy minibook Family Jesus Time.*)*

We're going to see if we can spread a secret word around the whole church just by whispering it to two people. Surely this is impossible!

Whisper an easy word like 'picnic' to two people and tell them to whisper it to two more people. Those four people can whisper it to two people each: how long does it take before everyone in the church has heard the secret word? Can you all shout it at once? You might want to try it again with a different word to see if you can do it any faster. And yes, some people hear the word wrong and some people share the wrong word on purpose (which is quite funny all the same), so that makes it all the more important to tell not just one person, not just two people, but as many people as we can all about Jesus.

Jesus had come back from the dead, proving that he really was God. But only a tiny number of people knew that. This was God's secret to share with the whole world. Jesus gave the job of passing on the good news, not to two of his disciples but to eleven of them. Imagine if each of them had told just two people, who had told just two people, who had told just two people… I wonder if the good news about Jesus would have spread as far as us, in a very far away country thousands of years later. The way new disciples are made is by old disciples – whether you're five years old or 95 years old – sharing the good news of Jesus with people we meet. We need to share it with older people who might have been missed out and with younger people who haven't had the chance to hear it yet. Who can you share the good news about Jesus with this month?

Prayer

The best way to start sharing the good news is by asking Jesus to help us. Sit very quietly, if you can, for just a moment and ask Jesus to bring into your mind the name of one person he'd like you to pray for.

Let's pray for those people together.

Loving Jesus, thank you for the people you've put on our minds right now. Help us to be good friends to them and share the good news about you when the time is right. Amen

Song suggestions

- 'We're on this road' – Fischy Music
- 'Sing a new song' – Fischy Music
- 'One shall tell another' – Graham Kendrick

Meal suggestion

Hotdogs, beans and carrot sticks

Messy Extra

Acts 3:11–16; 4:1–4:
Lots of people hear about Jesus

Read the story together, reminding people what happened with the healing in Acts 3:1–11 last time.

- What do you find most interesting?
- What word or phrase stands out for you?
- What made more people believe in Jesus?
- What do you most admire about Peter and John?
- What difference will this story make this week in the way you talk about Jesus?

Activity

Decorate biscuits with designs that go with some aspect of this story (for example, prison bars, a mouth speaking, dots representing 5,000 people).

Prayer

Light candles or tealights, naming before God the people you want to hear about Jesus.

4

Sharing Resources

[Jesus said,] 'When the Son of Man comes in his glory, and all the angels with him, then he will sit on the throne of his glory. All the nations will be gathered before him, and he will separate people one from another as a shepherd separates the sheep from the goats, and he will put the sheep at his right hand and the goats at the left. Then the king will say to those at his right hand, "Come, you that are blessed by my Father, inherit the kingdom prepared for you from the foundation of the world; for I was hungry and you gave me food, I was thirsty and you gave me something to drink, I was a stranger and you welcomed me, I was naked and you gave me clothing, I was sick and you took care of me, I was in prison and you visited me."

'Then the righteous will answer him, "Lord, when was it that we saw you hungry and gave you food, or thirsty and gave you something to drink? And when was it that we saw you a stranger and welcomed you, or naked and gave you clothing? And when was it that we saw you sick or in prison and visited you?"

'And the king will answer them, "Truly I tell you, just as you did it to one of the least of these who are members of my family, you did it to me." Then he will say to those at his left hand, "You that are accursed, depart from me into the eternal fire prepared for the devil and his angels; for I was hungry and you gave me no food, I was thirsty and you gave me nothing to drink, I was a stranger and you did not welcome me, naked and you did not give me clothing, sick and in prison and you did not visit me."

'Then they also will answer, "Lord, when was it that we saw you hungry or thirsty or a stranger or naked or sick or in prison, and did not take care of you?"

'Then he will answer them, "Truly I tell you, just as you did not do it to one of the least of these, you did not do it to me." And these will go away into eternal punishment, but the righteous into eternal life.'

MATTHEW 25:31–46

#discipleship

Messy team theme

- Who do you have on your team who shares something to make (Messy) church happen so well? Say thank you for them and to them.
- What surprising object do you each own that you'd be happy to lend out occasionally?
- What's the biggest thing you've ever been lent?

How does this session help people grow in Christ?

The early followers of Jesus were countercultural in the way they shared their possessions with each other. They seemed to have a very healthy, generous attitude to their belongings, and God used this to demonstrate to the wider community that these Jesus-people were putting their money where their mouth was. It was proof that they really believed what they were saying. It must also have helped them realise that what had previously been so apparently vital for life – status, relationships, etc. – was actually worthless in comparison with knowing Jesus and being part of his kingdom-building 'team'. They held tightly to Christ and lightly to everything around them: a very liberating way to live, especially in a materialistic society.

Mealtime card

- When have you ever worn a disguise?
- When have you met someone in a disguise?
- What difference would it make if you knew Jesus was disguised as people at school, work or in your family?

Take-home idea

This month, see if you can fill in every day of a calendar with one thing someone in the family has managed to share with others that day. It can be as small as you like: the idea is to get into practice!

Question to start and end the session

So… are we grabbers or sharers?

Activities

1 Sort the sheep

You will need: printed cards of goats and sheep (download online); a timer

Shuffle the cards and put them in a pile face down. See if you can sort the sheep from the goats inside a minute! Put the sheep on the right and the goats on the left.

Talk about how Middle-Eastern sheep and goats can look quite similar at first glance. A shepherd would be able to sort them, but some of us might find it tricky. In Jesus' parable, the sorting is done according to what people have done to other people. How does Jesus want us to treat other people?

2 Sharing platter

You will need: snacks, such as dips, crisps, vegetables, fruit, dried fruit and so on; flat platters; herbs for garnishing; little dishes

Create some beautiful sharing platters of nibbles for the mealtime. Be very visible about hygiene if you want adults to eat anything that's created. Arrange snacks and dips decoratively on a platter to share. Make each one into a work of art.

Talk about how Jesus said in his parable that the 'sheep' gave him something to eat when he was hungry – by feeding 'one of the least of these who are members of my family'. Who can you help with food today, or perhaps further afield than just at Messy Church?

3 Thirsty candle

You will need: a candle; a plate; coloured water; matches; a glass that fits over the candle

Cover the plate with coloured water a few millimetres deep. Stand the candle in the water and light it. Place the glass over the top of the candle so its rim is standing in the water. Watch what happens as it burns up all the oxygen. (Water gets 'sucked' into the glass, making it look as if the candle is thirsty! What really happens is the air pressure gets lower as the oxygen is used up by the flame, so the liquid is drawn into the lower pressure space inside the glass.)

Talk about what it feels like to be really thirsty. Which charities/not-for-profits work to help people have safe drinking water? What do you think Jesus would think of them?

4 Welcome sign

You will need: hanging slate shapes (relatively cheap from craft suppliers); liquid chalk pens (quite expensive so it's worth co-operating with your local Messy Churches to share the resources and the cost)

Decorate a sign to hang by your front door to welcome your guests.

Talk about how, in the parable, Jesus mentions he knows the 'sheep' by the way they welcome strangers. What might this mean to you, when 'stranger danger' is a real thing? What strangers might you make welcome?

5 Clothes

You will need: apron template on paper (download online, or draw around a children's apron); pens; for the adult version: old jeans, sewing scissors, pins, sewing machine and thread or nappy pins; for the easy version: newspaper, paper scissors, sticky tape

Fold your apron template in half lengthways and place the fold against the inside leg seam at the bottom of a leg of an old pair of jeans. Cut out the pattern shape and open out into the full apron shape. Cut off seams from the jeans to form the straps for the neck and the two waist ties. Either sew them on with the sewing machine or use large nappy pins to hold them in place.

The easy version can be made using a broadsheet newspaper and the same pattern, taping on the ties and neck piece.

Talk about how, in the parable, Jesus recognised his sheep because they had given clothes to people who needed them. How can we be responsible in the way we buy and use clothes?

6 Thinking of you sheep

You will need: felting wool; tea towels; water; liquid soap; googly eyes; black funky foam or card; glue; postcard or card; glue dots

Make a sheep's body by felting a ball of wool. Stretch out the wool until it is evenly spread. Putting a tea towel down to protect your table, gently wet your wool and add a little soap, then gently move it from hand to hand, using your fingers as a cage. Allow five minutes or so for the fibres to felt down, before you start squeezing and pressing the ball together more firmly into a compact globe. Rinse thoroughly. Squeeze out the water and allow to dry. Make a face from black funky foam or card and glue on two eyes, then glue the face to the front of the ball. Glue on to a postcard and give it to someone who is housebound or in hospital to let them know you're thinking of them.

Talk about what difference it might make to someone if you visited them or sent them a card (or a sheep!) when they were under the weather. What better way to show someone you love them? Do you think it's also a way of showing that you love Jesus?

7 Prison

You will need: blank postcards; coloured pens; access to the website or magazine of an organisation that works to release prisoners who are incarcerated unjustly (for example, Amnesty International)

Design and write cheerful postcards to be sent to people in prison to give them hope and a feeling of connection. You can gather these up afterwards and do the hard work of addressing and posting them.

Talk about how you would feel if Jesus was in your local prison. What would you want to do about it? What does Jesus mean when he says, 'Just as you did it to one of the least of these who are members of my family, you did it to me.'

8 Sharing the light

You will need: matches; candles in sturdy candleholders; a sand tray or foil covering for the table; tapers (optional)

Light one candle, then invite someone to light a second candle from the first one. But, before they do it, ask if they think the first candle will go out as it passes its flame on to the second one. What if you light a third candle from the first one? Or from the second one? Surely the first candle flame must get smaller if you share it round three, four or five candles? (Younger members might be given a taper to move the flame from one to another, rather than lifting the candle itself.)

Talk about how amazing it is that the light is shared around so generously and doesn't make the light of the first candle any smaller! When we share our resources with other people, do we necessarily lose them? What resources do we still have even when we give them away? (Love, hugs, smiles, words of comfort, affirmation and actions of helpfulness are all examples of us giving out and not having any less.) Are they like the candle flame, perhaps, that can be passed on endlessly, lighting up the world with the love that was lit in us by Jesus?

9 Paintbrushes to share

You will need: strong twigs; natural objects, such as leaves, grass stems, flowers, feathers, lichen; string; scissors; paint; paper

Make an interesting paintbrush to lend or give to someone older or younger than you who can't do this activity because they haven't got the time, skill or desire to do it. Take a small selection of natural objects and bind them tightly to one end of a twig using the string, to make a natural paintbrush. Experiment with different objects to see which makes the most effective paintbrush.

Talk about how hard it was to spend a while making this paintbrush with a lot of care, then giving it away to someone else. How did it feel? Would it have been any easier to give it away to Jesus himself?

10 Photo-booth disguises

You will need: hats; moustaches; beards; spectacles; scarves; eye-masks and other disguises; make-up (optional); a large cardboard box or frame to make into a photo booth; a camera or phone and the means to transfer the pictures on to a laptop to display them

(Make sure you have consent for photos.) Invite people to disguise themselves to look as different as possible and to have a photo taken of themselves in the photo booth. Display all the photos during the celebration or meal and see if you can guess who they are.

Talk about how, in the parable, there's a lot of disguise going on. The sheep and the goats look very similar to each other. And Jesus himself seems to be disguised as 'one of the least of these who are members of my family' so well that the sheep are surprised to hear they've actually been sharing what they have with Jesus, not just with people.

Celebration

Start by showing a clip from the film Finding Nemo *that starts with Gerald the pelican in Sydney Harbour choking on Marlin and Dory and finishes as Nigel the pelican successfully flies away with the two fish in his beak, leaving the seagulls stuck in the sail of the yacht (about 1'35").*

What word is used most often in that clip? Of course, it's the simple 'Mine' from every single seagull. Does anyone think that some of us are a bit like that, greedily wanting to grab and hold on to things and make everything 'mine'? Look at the chaos and disaster that happens when so many seagulls live by the word and attitude, 'Mine'!

Interestingly, did you know the pelican is an ancient Christian symbol for Jesus?*

Jesus wants his disciples to live a different way. He tells a strange parable – a story with secrets – about a king sorting out a herd of animals. (*Start acting it out.*) Sheep on the right, goats on the left, sheep on the right, goats on the left. You're a sheep – go right. You're a goat – go left. Sheep, right. Goat, left.

Right! All you sheep! Come this way! I've got a wonderful party ready for you to say thank you for looking after me! Do you remember? 'I was hungry and you gave me something to eat, I was thirsty and you gave me something to drink, I was a stranger and you invited me in, I needed clothes and you clothed me, I was ill and you looked after me, I was in prison and you came to visit me.'

But the sheep were confused. They said, 'Your majesty, when did we see you hungry and feed you, or thirsty and give you something to drink? When did we see you a stranger and invite you in, or needing clothes and clothe you? When did we see you ill or in prison and go to visit you?'

The king replied, 'Whatever you did for one of the least of these brothers and sisters of mine, you did for me' (see Matthew 25:35–40, NIV).

Sadly, the goats were the ones who had seen people in need and had held on to their food, drink, homes, spare clothes, time and effort, saying, 'Mine! Mine! Mine!', instead of sharing what they had, so they didn't get an invitation to the party.

Jesus wants everyone who follows him to learn about the party-feeling of sharing and to know it's the best way to live. The first people who followed Jesus understood this and shared everything they owned with each other. Instead of 'Mine! Mine! Mine!', they would say, 'Ours! Ours! Ours!'

Let's give it a try this month and see if it makes any difference to think of everything we have as 'ours' rather than 'mine'. I wonder what will be most difficult. I wonder what wonderful surprises will come our way.

(*People used to think the pelican fed its young from its own body, and early Christians thought this was like Jesus feeding us with his body in Holy Communion. Pelicans don't, but the symbol adds something to the meaning of the moment when the pelican in the film mutters, 'Hop inside my mouth if you want to live.')

Prayer

Have a set of pictures – a lunchbox, a water bottle, a front door, a coat, a clock. Ask two leaders to be the goats and everyone else to be sheep. As each picture is shown, say:

Here's some _____. The goats say…

Leaders: 'Mine! Mine! Mine!'

But the sheep say…

All: 'Ours! Ours! Ours!'

Repeat for all the pictures. (Here's some food… Here's some drink… Here's a welcome… Here's some clothing … Here's 24 hours in the day…)

Jesus, help us to practise this really hard thing of sharing what we have with each other so your world becomes a sharing place, not a grabbing place. Amen

Song suggestions

- 'Build up' – Fischy Music
- 'God forgave my sin in Jesus' name' – Alliance Media Ltd

Meal suggestion

Sharing platters as above

Messy Extra

Acts 4:32–37: Sharing everything!

Read the story together.

- What do you find most interesting?
- What word or phrase stands out for you?
- Why do you think the early Jesus-followers did this as much as they seem to have done?
- Do you think this attitude would 'work' today in your church?
- What difference will this story make this week in the way you choose to worship Jesus?

Activity

Try to devise a game called 'Reverse Monopoly', using the same boardgame but trying to make sure everybody has a similar amount of money and property by the end of the game. What rules do you have to change?

Prayer

Using wool or string, tie a small object like a box to everybody's hand – you'll need to help each other. Reflect for a moment how attached we all are to our possessions. Ask God to release us all from being too attached, just as you now cut the bonds with a pair of scissors.

5

Serving

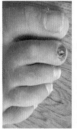

Now before the festival of the Passover, Jesus knew that his hour had come to depart from this world and go to the Father. Having loved his own who were in the world, he loved them to the end. The devil had already put it into the heart of Judas son of Simon Iscariot to betray him.

And during supper Jesus, knowing that the Father had given all things into his hands, and that he had come from God and was going to God, got up from the table, took off his outer robe, and tied a towel around himself. Then he poured water into a basin and began to wash the disciples' feet and to wipe them with the towel that was tied around him. He came to Simon Peter, who said to him, 'Lord, are you going to wash my feet?' Jesus answered, 'You do not know now what I am doing, but later you will understand.' Peter said to him, 'You will never wash my feet.' Jesus answered, 'Unless I wash you, you have no share with me.' Simon Peter said to him, 'Lord, not my feet only but also my hands and my head!' Jesus said to him, 'One who has bathed does not need to wash, except for the feet, but is entirely clean. And you are clean, though not all of you.' For he knew who was to betray him; for this reason he said, 'Not all of you are clean.'

After he had washed their feet, had put on his robe, and had returned to the table, he said to them, 'Do you know what I have done to you? You call me Teacher and Lord – and you are right, for that is what I am. So if I, your Lord and Teacher, have washed your feet, you also ought to wash one another's feet. For I have set you an example, that you also should do as I have done to you. Very truly, I tell you, servants are not greater than their master, nor are messengers greater than the one who sent them. If you know these things, you are blessed if you do them.

JOHN 13:1–17

#discipleship

Messy team theme

- What do you love about serving others through your Messy Church?
- How do you think your team is reflecting Christ by the way you all serve others?
- Is there any danger of Christlike servanthood becoming unhelpful martyrdom?

How does this session help people grow in Christ?

As he washes his disciples' feet, Jesus models for every one of his followers what leadership means. Whether we lead a family, a group or a team at work or school, Jesus' example of deliberately laying aside power in order to make life better for others is one we can all follow. If a whole Messy Church-load of people of all ages went into their community filled with the desire to serve others and put them first, what a difference that would make to our world!

Mealtime card

- When were your feet the smelliest they've ever been?
- Who has served you today?
- Who could you serve tomorrow?

Take-home idea

Do the five-minute servant hat challenge. Find a hat (or apron or any item of clothing) and take it in turns to wear the hat and be everyone's servant in your family for just five minutes. For five minutes, you have to do just what you are asked to do (as long as it's safe, legal, doesn't include any of your property and can be achieved in five minutes. Your brother telling you to go out and spend all your money on cans of drink for him, for example, is not within the rules. And anyway, if he wants to have a servant for five minutes, he must also be a servant for five minutes himself.)

Question to start and end the session

So… is anyone too important to serve others?

Activities

1 Foot-painting

You will need: face paints; means of washing and drying feet

Invite people to have their feet painted instead of the more usual face or hands. Start by washing and drying the foot, then paint on a design. Invite them to suggest what Jesus' disciples might have trodden in on their way to the last supper, and paint that on. Squashed grapes, mud, dust and donkey dung are just a few suggestions to inspire creativity.

Talk about how horrible the disciples' feet must have been at the last supper and how they would have had someone else's feet almost in their face as they reclined around the table together. What might that have been like? Why didn't anyone do something about it?

2 Toenail art

You will need: nail varnish; accessories

Invite people to have one toenail painted to remind them of the last supper. Add nail accessories if wanted. As you paint the nail, tell the story of the foot-washing.

Talk about how nail bars are known to have many trafficked people working in them: modern-day slaves. In Jesus' time, slaves were the ones to wash people's feet. How aware of modern-day slavery are we? Would raising awareness of it be a good way of serving our neighbours?

3 Tissue aid

You will need: felt; needles; threads; scissors; beads, sequins, etc.; glue; tissues; sewing machine (optional)

Cut out 7" by 6" rectangles of felt. Fold to the middle along the long edge so that both long edges meet in the middle, making a slit. Sew across each short end of the rectangle. Trim the excess felt from the short ends.

Decorate with felt, beads or sequins, glued or sewn on. Tuck in some tissues and ease the edge out of the slit.

Talk about how you might use these tissues to help other people. Your challenge is to use each of these tissues to serve someone else, by giving them away at just the right time when someone needs one. Talk about the way Jesus showed his disciples how they, too, should be ready to do the dirtiest jobs to make life better for other people, when he washed their feet.

4 Climbing the ladder

You will need: photos of famous people and people from your Messy Church or local community; a large picture of a ladder or staircase on a sheet of paper; map pins (if you're doing it vertically)

Invite people to put the photos on the ladder in order of who is the most important, with the most important at the top of the ladder. Feel free to rearrange them and talk about why they are at the top, bottom or in the middle.

Talk about whether there are things that really important people shouldn't be expected to do for themselves or for others. Why did Jesus choose to do the most menial job possible when he washed his disciples' feet? If you were really important/famous/rich/well known, would you want to serve others or be served?

5 Make a toe spa

You will need: drinking straws; pencils; paper bowls; water; bubble bath; towels; floor covering; more towels

Make a hole (using a pencil) in the bowl near the rim through which to poke a straw. Put as much water in the bowl as you dare and add a squirt of bubble bath. Invite a friend or long-suffering parent to enjoy a toe spa (the budget doesn't run to a foot spa). They put one toe in the bowl and you blow vigorously into the straw to make bubbles. This might be messy.

Talk about how Jesus washed his disciples' feet in order to show them how they should always serve other people and put others first. What can we do this week to put others first?

6 Fruit foot (or froot fuit)

You will need: fruit of different sorts, including grapes, small berries or raisins and slices of fruit like a cross section of a pear, apple, banana or pineapple; plates; pureed berries

Use the pureed berries as glue to stick pieces of fruit on to a plate to make a foot or footprint shape out of fruit. Eat the fruit foot before it goes brown.

Talk about why Jesus washed his friends' feet. What did he have to give up to serve others in this way? The early church people gave up their money to serve others who were in need. Is there something we could give up to serve others?

7 Smelly sock contest

You will need: old socks steeped in different liquids or containing different solids

Number the socks and invite people to sniff them to work out what they smell of. (You will have your own ideas but suggestions include vinegar, talc, mint, popcorn, rosemary, curry, pine, wood shavings, grass clippings, chocolate and, if you have access to it, horse or cow dung has a splendid fragrance.) Who can guess the most?

Talk about how washing feet was a very unpleasant slave's job, as people's feet have never been very pleasant to sniff. Who does an unpleasant or dangerous job to make life better for other people?

8 Foot scrub

You will need: Vaseline; ethically sourced palm oil or coconut oil; oatmeal; coarse salt; essential oils or gentler flavours, such as mint leaves, rosemary leaves or lemon juice; bowls; spoons; small jars with lids

Mix up ingredients in a trial-and-error sort of way, experimenting with the amount you need to make a coarse scrub for feet that smells nice. Put it in the jar to take home.

Talk about how you might serve someone in your family by giving them a gentle foot massage with your foot scrub – in the bathroom or outside, not on the lounge carpet – and rinse it off at the end.

9 Sock rabbit

You will need: old socks; rice or sand; string; ribbon; scissors; marker pens

Carefully fill the toe and heel of the sock with rice or sand and shake it down so it's nice and full. Tie a piece of string about 3/4 of the way up the sock's full foot to make the rabbit's neck and again tie the top of the head tightly. Cut two ears out of the leg of the sock and trim off the extra fabric. Tie a ribbon round its neck and draw on two eyes, a nose and whiskers.

Talk about how we wear socks most of the year, but in Jesus' time socks weren't a thing and feet got very dirty. Was there any better way for Jesus to show us that he needs us all to be ready to do the dirty jobs on earth if that helps others? This rabbit gives us the '*hop*portunity' to remember to help other people.

10 Helpful shoelaces

You will need: pairs of coloured or white shoelaces; marker pens; beads; charms

Invite everyone to decorate a pair of shoelaces with drawn-on patterns and threaded-on beads or charms (knot them into place at one end of the lace).

Talk about the way these laces in our shoes can remind us that Jesus washed his friends' feet to serve them. He wants us to serve other people whenever we get the chance.

Celebration

Who's the most important person you've ever met?

Who's the most important person in your school or workplace?

Who's the most important person in this room? Who's the most important person in the world?

To his disciples, Jesus was the most important person in the universe! He had shown them he was not only a great leader but something even greater. His miracles and signs showed them he was God. The disciples were delighted to be his special friends: they had loved being cheered on with palm branches like the procession of a king the previous Sunday. And they looked forward to Jesus taking over the whole kingdom this very weekend. They were going to be princes and grand viziers and members of parliament and grand high governors and all the other wonderful powerful positions you get when you're friends with a king!

They gathered together in a room in a house in Jerusalem to celebrate the story of God's rescue years before, as they did every year with family and friends.

They'd all been out in the city all day. It was dusty. It was hot. There were donkeys and goats and camels and sheep – it was VERY dirty on the roads. And as they lay down on their sides around the table, as they always did for a meal, everyone became uncomfortably aware that there was a bit of a pong coming from their neighbour's feet, which were just under their nose. Phew! It was a warm evening and the smell got stronger. Phaw! Nobody had sorted out a servant to come and wash everyone's feet, as they always did. The bowl was there, the water was there and the towel was there, but no servant. And none of the disciples was going to do it. They were all too important! It should be someone unimportant to do the dirtiest job of the evening. And so they were just going to have to put up with it… phwergh!

But just then, Jesus got up, knotted the towel round his waist, poured water into the bowl, picked it up and knelt down. Then he washed his friends' feet one by one and dried them with the towel.

Nobody knew what to say. Jesus was the most important person in the room and there he was, doing the muckiest job. They were very, very uncomfortable. What did that say about Jesus? He shouldn't have done something so embarrassing: he was letting them all down… wasn't he?

At the end, Jesus sat down again and shocked them even more. 'Do you understand what I have done for you?' he asked them. 'You call me "Teacher" and "Lord", and rightly so, for that is what I am. Now that I, your Lord and Teacher, have washed your feet, you also should wash one another's feet. I have set you an example that you should do as I have done for you' (John 13:12–15, NIV).

What an amazing man! What an amazing God! What amazing things does he want us, his followers, to do to be like him? I don't think we need to actually wash anyone's feet, but what might they need us to do for them? Can you think of a way you can help someone else this week? Talk to the person you came with.

Any suggestions?

Prayer

Let's turn our story and our thoughts into a prayer.

Dear Jesus, you are the most important person on earth, but you chose to do the dirtiest job to serve others. Help us this week to serve other people and to be on the lookout for ways to make the world a better place. Let your kingdom come through us. Amen

Song suggestions

- 'Creativity' – Fischy Music
- 'Build up' – Fischy Music
- 'Brother, sister let me serve you' – Richard A.M. Gillard

Meal suggestion

Jacket potatoes, beans and cheese

Messy Extra

Acts 6: The first Jesus-followers look after the neighbourhood

Read the story together.

- What do you find most interesting?
- What word or phrase stands out for you?
- How do you think the widows found out that Jesus-followers were giving away food?
- Who is there in your neighbourhood who is in any way like the widows here?
- What does this story inspire you to do, say or pray?
- What difference will this story make this week in your walk with Jesus?

Activity

Make and bake pizzas together.

Prayer

Spread out a map of your area, and pray for the different buildings, community groups and streets which you see there.

6

Biblical Teaching

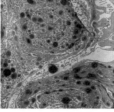
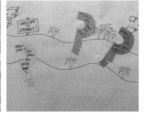

Now on that same day two of them were going to a village called Emmaus, about seven miles from Jerusalem, and talking with each other about all these things that had happened. While they were talking and discussing, Jesus himself came near and went with them, but their eyes were kept from recognising him. And he said to them, 'What are you discussing with each other while you walk along?' They stood still, looking sad.

Then one of them, whose name was Cleopas, answered him, 'Are you the only stranger in Jerusalem who does not know the things that have taken place there in these days?' He asked them, 'What things?' They replied, 'The things about Jesus of Nazareth, who was a prophet mighty in deed and word before God and all the people, and how our chief priests and leaders handed him over to be condemned to death and crucified him. But we had hoped that he was the one to redeem Israel. Yes, and besides all this, it is now the third day since these things took place. Moreover, some women of our group astounded us. They were at the tomb early this morning, and when they did not find his body there, they came back and told us that they had indeed seen a vision of angels who said that he was alive. Some of those who were with us went to the tomb and found it just as the women had said; but they did not see him.'

Then he said to them, 'Oh, how foolish you are, and how slow of heart to believe all that the prophets have declared! Was it not necessary that the Messiah should suffer these things and then enter into his glory?' Then beginning with Moses and all the prophets, he interpreted to them the things about himself in all the scriptures.

As they came near the village to which they were going, he walked ahead as if he were going on. But they urged him strongly, saying, 'Stay with us, because it is almost evening and the day is now nearly over.' So he went in to stay with them. When he was at the table with them, he took bread, blessed and broke it, and gave it to them. Then their eyes were opened, and they recognised him; and he vanished from their sight. They said to each other, 'Were not our hearts burning within us while he was talking to us on the road, while he was opening the scriptures to us?' That same hour they got up and returned to Jerusalem; and they found the eleven

> and their companions gathered together. They were saying, 'The Lord
> has risen indeed, and he has appeared to Simon!' Then they told what
> had happened on the road, and how he had been made known to them
> in the breaking of the bread.
>
> LUKE 24:13–35

#discipleship

Messy team theme

- What do we find helpful to understand the Bible better?
- If we were marooned on a desert island, which book of the Bible would we most like to have?
- Which image of God's word do we like best (honey, light, bread, sword, etc.)?

How does this session help people grow in Christ?

Every Messy Church explores the Bible, so this session takes a step back and considers why this book of books is so important to the church, what we can expect to find in it and how it might affect our daily life. It also touches on tools people find helpful to understand the Bible better.

Mealtime card

- What's your favourite story about Jesus?
- If you haven't got a Bible at home, would you like one?
- If you have got a Bible, where is it kept?

Take-home idea

This month, try reading one Bible story every day at bedtime. Ask your church if there's a family Bible or children's Bible you could use, if you don't have one of your own.

Question to start and end the session

So… why bother with the Bible?

Activities

1 Minute to win it

You will need: about 20 large, brightly coloured cards with the name of a book of the Bible written on it; a timer; a Bible open at the contents page

Give each competitor one minute to arrange six of the cards into the correct order as found in the Bible. If they're really good at it, see how many books they can put in the right order in a minute. If they're very challenged by it, because of age or not being able to read, give lots of clues and help.

Talk about the way the Bible is made up of 66 different books, inspired by God and written by people. What do you think the Bible is for? Why does the church think the Bible is so important?

2 Bible study suitcase

You will need: instruction diagrams (download online); plastic milk bottles; marker pens; scissors; Velcro or fastener; washi tape or electrical tape; Bible booklets; Post-it notes

Make a plastic suitcase: draw the shape on the milk bottle as shown in the instructions, then cut out along the line. Fold the long end down over the gap. Add a fastener to close it. Cover the edges with coloured tape.

Invite people to put inside the suitcase a Bible booklet and a small stack of Post-it notes. Use the Post-it notes to mark special moments on the pages that you don't want to forget, as you read it.

Talk about how the two travellers in today's story would have had the ancient equivalent of suitcases as they travelled back to Emmaus from Jerusalem. But the person they met on the road didn't need a suitcase for his Bible: he had the Bible in his heart and knew it word for word! Do you like learning things by heart? Which parts of the Bible would you like to learn and carry with you always? Stories about Jesus? Some of the things he said? Poetry?

3 Memory game

You will need: items to do with finding your way, such as a compass, map, satnav, phone, torch, signpost, globe, star, arrow/pointer, picture of a road sign; a tray

Give people a set amount of time to observe the items on your tray, then ask them to close their eyes while you remove one or more of them. They then look at the tray and try to work out what you've removed.

Talk about what helps you find your way on a journey. Some of these things might. As we find our way through life, God gives us the Bible to help us find our way through difficult situations, and the Holy Spirit to help us come closer to Jesus through good times and bad. When have you used the Bible to help you work out the best choice to make?

4 Honey words

You will need: runny honey (or fruit puree if you're anxious about sugar intake); cotton buds; paper plates; pencils

Write in big letters a word on a plate that describes the Bible (such as light, bread, sword, living, active, Jesus, word, truth, Logos). Then write over the top of the letters in honey/puree, using the cotton bud as a pen. You can lick the honey/puree off with your tongue!

This is how Jewish children used to learn to read and write, which might be why one of the psalms says, 'How sweet are your words to my taste, sweeter than honey to my mouth!' (Psalm 119:103).

Talk about how a book can be 'sweet' like honey. How did hearing the Bible explained make a difference to Cleopas and his friend? How did their mood and outlook change?

5 Clean messy painting

You will need: cling film; paint; a large tray (optional)

Pour paint on to the table (or into a large tray if you're nervous). Stretch cling film over the top of it. Invite people to think of a story from the Bible and draw it with a finger in the paint through the cling film and see if others can guess what story it is. Give them clues if you need to.

Talk about how, when Cleopas and his friend were sad because they didn't understand why Jesus had to die, Jesus himself explained God's plan as it was set out in the Bible: he gave them the big picture. The Bible helps us see that God has a big plan, even if the part we're going through at the moment is difficult.

6 A lighthouse

You will need: the means to make a circuit; a light bulb; a battery

Enjoy creating circuits to light up the bulb. Talk about the way the power needs to flow around a complete circuit to light it up. The psalmist wrote that God's word is like 'a lamp to my feet' (Psalm 119:105). Jesus described himself as 'the light of the world' (John 8:12).

Talk about how Cleopas and his friend had some parts of the circuit, but needed Jesus to complete the circuit and make the light shine so they really understood God's plan. We need to ask for Jesus' help when we find Bible stories we don't understand fully.

7 Mind the gap marbling

You will need: marbling inks; water; a shallow tray; paper; pens; masking tape (optional); a hairdryer (optional); copies of Bible verses (download online)

Float marbling inks on the surface of your water, but don't stir them in quite as much as you normally might – leave the blobs of ink fairly substantial so that when you peel off the paper from the water, there are areas of white space between the marbling. (If you can't make it work, you could mask off areas with masking tape before you marble.) Dry the paper with the hairdryer or leave it to dry naturally, then copy one or more key Bible verses into the white spaces in an attractive way.

Talk about how we don't have Jesus physically walking next to us to explain the Bible, but we can meet with each other to explore it. Have you ever thought of joining a church group to read the Bible and ask questions about it?

8 Emmaus roadmap

You will need: a big sheet of paper with the Emmaus road sketched out on it; large question-mark shapes in coloured paper; pens; glue; paint; brushes

Invite people to think of a question they would have asked Jesus if they'd been Cleopas, walking along the road with Jesus. Write the question on a question mark shape and glue it to the road scene. Use paints to paint in the background scenery as you talk through how you might find an answer to your question.

Talk about the different ways you have found it helpful to explore the Bible.

9 Bible reading challenge

You will need: a Bible reading challenge poster (download online); a set of seven stickers; coloured pens

Are you up for the Bible reading challenge?! Colour in your poster and over the coming week, each time you manage to read the day's Bible story, give yourselves a sticker on the poster!

Talk about how lots of Christians read the Bible every day to make sure they're listening to God all the time, whatever they feel like.

10 Matchbox surprise

You will need: matchboxes or very small boxes with lids; strips of paper; sticky tape; coloured pens

Write out a concise version of Jesus' summary of the scriptures on the strip of paper: 'Love the Lord your God with all your heart and with all your soul and with all your mind and love your neighbour as yourself.' Concertina the strip using small sharp folds, and tape it into the matchbox so that it pops up when you open the box. Decorate the outside of the box to look like a very small Bible.

Talk about how Jesus didn't have a very long time to explain God's whole plan to Cleopas. Sometimes it's good to think about the huge, big story of God (like the summary in your little box) and sometimes it's good to think about just one story from the Bible in a lot of detail. We have time to do both!

Celebration

Stage a game of hide and seek between a couple of the leaders.

Sometimes it feels as if Jesus is playing hide and seek with us! We might have questions about what's going on around us and Jesus feels nowhere near to answer them. But he did make his friends a promise: 'Seek and you *will* find.' If we keep on looking and asking, we *will* find the answer; we *will* find where Jesus is hiding – like Cleopas and his friend in our story today.

Cleopas and his friend were feeling very down and were full of sad questions. They'd just seen their best friend Jesus killed on a cross, and they'd thought that everything they believed in was at an end. They thought they'd got it completely wrong and that Jesus was just a human being, not God at all. But then these rumours started up that people had actually seen Jesus alive again. Cleopas and his friend were feeling very down and full of sad questions. They decided to leave the city and walk home to Emmaus to get away from it all.

And as they walked along, feeling down and full of sad questions, someone came up beside them and asked them why they looked so down and sad. They told him what the matter was. But the stranger laughed and told them they were daft! 'Don't you see this had to happen?' he said. And as they walked along together, he explained to them what the scriptures said about God's big plan for the world and how it all came together in Jesus' dying and rising again. And as they walked along together, Cleopas and his friend started looking up and asking questions and laughing at the wonderful answers and seeing that everything they'd believed about Jesus was true and that it was even better than they'd thought!

As they got to their house, the stranger with so many answers and so many questions looked as if he was about to keep on walking, but Cleopas and his friend made him come in for a meal. As they sat down to eat, the stranger lifted up the bread to bless it, and suddenly Cleopas and his friend recognised that it wasn't a stranger at all; it was Jesus himself, alive and full of life and liveliness. But just as they recognised him, he disappeared. It was like a game of hide and seek! They were so full of excitement and questions and answers that they dropped everything and ran back to the city to find the other disciples. 'We've seen Jesus!' they shouted, all out of breath. 'So have we!' said the others. 'So have we!'

Cleopas and his friend knew scripture really well, but they still didn't understand it all. They needed Jesus to come and help them see what it was all about.

I wonder what questions we have about the Bible. Let's have a look at some of them from our big artwork… (*Read out some answers to activity 8.*) What great questions! Let's keep on looking for the answers. Some of us might find it helpful to read a little bit of the Bible every day. Some of us might want to look at the stories in a children's Bible. Some might want to join a group to find out more of what God has to say in the Bible to life's big questions. If you'd like to find out more, have a word with [*name of a leader*] afterwards. And for all of us, let's remember the more we seek, the more we will find, as Jesus promised.

Prayer

Invite two or three people to hide around the room and be ready to jump out of their hiding places when you raise your hands.

Jesus, sometimes trying to understand your plan for us is like being the seeker in a game of hide and seek. We search and search and search through the wonderful stories, poetry and laws in the Bible… and it takes so long… and we feel like giving up. And we try just one more time… and (*raise your hands*) there you are! Help us to keep seeking you in your wonderful world, in the wonderful people around us and in your wonderful word, the Bible. Amen

Song suggestions

- 'Written on the palm of God's hand' – Fischy Music
- 'When people are cruel' – Fischy Music
- 'My lighthouse' – Rend Collective

Meal suggestion

Chicken or quorn in sauce, with rice and peas

Messy Extra

Acts 8:26–40: Philip and the Ethiopian

Read through the story together and, if you have the space to, act it out.

- Which word or phrase stands out? (Make a note of these for use in the prayer.)
- What other stories does this remind you of?
- What's different about this one?
- What do you like best in this story?
- What does this story tell us about studying scripture?
- What helps you in the habit of reading the Bible? If you don't read the Bible, what would you find useful to help you start?
- What one idea from this story will you take away to think about more this week?

Activity

Make chariots out of junk and have a chariot race.

Prayer

Look at the words and phrases you noticed in the passage when you read it. Try turning these into a prayer and saying it together.

7

Eating Together

> After this [Jesus] went out and saw a tax-collector named Levi, sitting at the tax booth; and he said to him, 'Follow me.' And he got up, left everything, and followed him.
>
> Then Levi gave a great banquet for him in his house; and there was a large crowd of tax-collectors and others sitting at the table with them. The Pharisees and their scribes were complaining to his disciples, saying, 'Why do you eat and drink with tax-collectors and sinners?' Jesus answered, 'Those who are well have no need of a physician, but those who are sick; I have come to call not the righteous but sinners to repentance.'
>
> LUKE 5:27–32

#discipleship

Messy team theme

- What's your favourite meal?
- What do you think you're doing when you eat together in Messy Church?
- When did you last eat together as a team?

How does this session help people grow in Christ?

The obvious holy habit to encourage in a Messy Church setting is that of eating together as a family. It's also good to invite those who aren't in families to eat with us to grow the kingdom, combat isolation and get to know each other better. We need to be careful not to make people feel guilty or inferior if they don't or can't eat together: just to invite people to enjoy this aspect of being a Jesus-follower.

Mealtime card

- What's the best thing about eating together?
- What's the funniest thing that's happened to you at a meal?
- What food reminds you of someone in your family who's a long way away?

Take-home idea

This month, light a candle at your meal table every day to remind you to say one thing to God before you eat.

Question to start and end the session

So… what's so great about eating together?

Activities

1 Prayer plate

You will need: plain plates; coloured marker pens

You can do this activity in different ways: you might decide to make one plate that everyone adds a decoration to. This plate could be used at Messy Church but sent home with a different family every month to use at home, especially if it has a prayer on it. Or you could make a plate per family.

Decorate a special plate to put out at family meals (Place a napkin on top of the plate and something like biscuits or cake on top of that.) You might write on a grace to say thank you for the meal you've just eaten. Or simply the words: 'Eat… pray… hug…'

To make the design semi-permanent, bake in the oven at home. Put the plates in the oven and set the temperature to 350F/180C/Gas Mark 4. Turn the oven off after 30 minutes and let the plates cool inside the oven.

Talk about the reason we eat together at Messy Church, which is to show we're like one big family in the church. Why do you think Jesus ate with people?

2 Great Messy Bake-Off

You will need: a simple recipe and its ingredients and equipment

Invite people to compete to make the Best Messy Whatever-It-Is. Have a suitably pompous judging time with people playing the parts of the TV show judges and compères.

Talk about how eating together is absolutely not about a competition to see who is the best cook. It's about loving people and showing this love by making a meal for them and inviting them into your home. Jesus ate with all sorts of people to show them how much he loved them just as they were.

3 Meal in a bag

You will need: bags; different things to fill the bags, depending on your circumstances; pens

This activity will vary depending on the needs of your community and on your financial resources. The basic idea is to create a take-home bag containing items that encourage a family to sit down to a meal together. At its simplest, the bag might contain a tealight and/or small flower arrangement as a centrepiece, a bar of chocolate to break into pieces and share after the meal, and a grace printed out on a card to say before the meal. But if you live in a needy area, you might want to provide ingredients and a recipe card for a simple meal, and a cake or some fruit to have for pudding. Decorate the bag with the instructions 'Meal in a bag! Just add love!'

Talk about what fun it is to sit down together and talk about the day you've just had while you eat. Jesus loved sharing food and time with people to show them how much he loved them.

4 Furniture

You will need: offcuts of wood with a hammer, nails and a saw, or an old table; acrylic paints; paint brushes; stencils

Make or upcycle a table.

Talk about the way we can gather round a table to eat a meal but also the table you may have in your church. What special meal do we have round that table? Who is invited to that special meal?

5 Who's welcome?

You will need: a prepared picture of a table with lots of place settings and blank name tags; paints; paint brushes; pens

Invite people to choose where to sit at this table and put their name in the name tag. Talk about who else Jesus wants at his table: what groups of people would he like to sit down and eat with? Put them on the name tags, too. Paint in the details of the table settings and add food to the plates and drink to the cups to make it look like a wonderful feast.

Talk about how some people thought Jesus was wrong to eat with 'dodgy' people and that it reflected badly on him. In today's story, the religious people told him he was wrong to eat with the tax collectors. What did Jesus reply?

6 Sorting contest

You will need: any collection that has lots of different colours or sizes or shapes, such as a box of buttons, beads or toy cars

Pile the items in the middle of the table and challenge two teams or individuals to see who can sort out the most of the category you tell them within one minute. Tell one team one category (e.g. 'All the red beads!') and the other team another (e.g. 'All the yellow beads!') and see who manages to take out most in one minute.

Talk about the way the religious leaders in Jesus' time wanted to sort out the good people from the bad people. They would never sit down and eat with 'bad' people because they might become bad themselves. But Jesus did something different. What did he do and why do you think he did it?

7 Table manners quiz

You will need: printouts of the quiz (download online); pens

Have fun with the quiz of table manners in different parts of the world.

Talk about what makes us feel safe when we sit down and eat with people we don't know very well. How safe would you feel sitting down to a meal with Jesus?

8 Butter-making

You will need: double cream; clean jars with lids; salt

Fill your jar about 1/5 full of double cream – and shake and shake and shake until it turns to butter. Add a little salt to taste. Take it to the Messy mealtime to eat on bread there.

Talk about how good it is to sit down and eat something you or someone in your family has made yourselves. A meal is a great way to show people you love them. What meals can you think of where Jesus sat and ate with someone?

9 Grow your own

You will need: pots; compost; lettuce (or other veg) seeds; labels to decorate; pens

Plant some seeds in a pot and plan to invite someone to come and eat the vegetable with you when it's ready. Write their name on the label to remind you. If the plant doesn't grow, perhaps you could invite that person for a meal anyway!

Talk about how Jesus invites anyone and everyone to come to his table. You don't need to be a good person. You just have to say yes to the invitation.

10 Badge-making

You will need: a badge-making machine (or stickers); paper; pens

Give everyone two badges to make: one that says, 'I'm invited!', and the other that says, 'You're invited!' Put a design on that shows something good about your Messy Church mealtime. Then wear one badge yourself and give the other away to someone who doesn't come to Messy Church yet, but who you would like to have there.

Talk about the mealtime in your Messy Church and what you enjoy about it. How much do you think Jesus enjoys it too?

Celebration

Play the part of Levi's next-door neighbour.

It's absolutely shocking!

That Jesus! They say he's the Son of God, but what does he do? He hangs out with the worst possible kind of person! I mean, would God want his Son to do that? I don't think so! God's Son would only spend time with good people. People who keep the rules. People like me, in fact!

I mean tonight – listen to that party going on next door! Music… dancing… bottles chinking… shouting and SO much laughter! Is that holy? I don't think so.

And do you know whose house it is? It belongs to Levi, one of the most criminal gangsters in town. He spends more time with the Romans than with his own people. He's a crook and a cheat and a materialistic money-grabbing swindler. But Jesus asked *him* to be one of his special friends! I mean! And because Levi was so happy to be picked out by the Son of God, he's gone and thrown a party for Jesus AND invited ALL his gangster friends. The street's been full of dodgy characters and their dodgy wives all night.

Perhaps Jesus is so daft he doesn't realise what sort of people they are? Perhaps – terrible thought – he actually LIKES being with people like Levi! Instead of with people like me, who always do the right thing and lead very good lives.

So I went next door to ask them to turn the music down a bit and said to him, 'Jesus, you want to watch yourself. You'll get a bad reputation if you sit down and eat with this sort of person. You should be in the synagogue being holy, not drinking and scoffing with these dreadful people. You don't belong here with them! Come and have a nice quiet sensible meal at my house and we can do some praying together.'

And he said to me, 'It's not healthy people that need a doctor, it's ill people. I haven't come to call people like you into a better life, but people like this.'

I don't know! Ridiculous! I mean, what sort of a God is this, who wants to give someone like Levi a second chance? I ask you! I wouldn't eat with Jesus – not in a million years. Would you?

Prayer

Give everyone a small sticky note. Display a picture of Levi's front door and his neighbour's front door on the same street. Invite people to spend a moment thinking whether they would like to sit down to a meal with Jesus or to a meal with that next-door neighbour we just met and to go and stick their sticky note on the door they've chosen.

Thank you, Jesus, that you love to sit down with us, whether we're all sorted and good or whether we're a bit of a mess. Help us to enjoy spending time with you and with each other now as we go into our Messy meal. Amen

Song suggestions

- 'E-N-J-O-Y' – Fischy Music
- 'Big family of God' – Nick and Becky Drake

Meal suggestion

Fishfingers, potato wedges and cucumber sticks

Messy Extra

Acts 9:1–19: Eating with the enemy

Read the story together.

- What word or phrase stands out for you?
- Why do you think this amazing passage ends with a meal?
- How do you think the other Jesus-followers felt about eating with Saul/Paul?
- Is there anyone you would find it hard to sit and eat a meal with? Why?
- What do you think about eating together as a group?
- What difference will this story make this week in your walk with Jesus?

Activity

Make electrical circuits out of potatoes or citrus fruits and talk about the power of food.

Prayer

Put a bowl of jelly babies in the centre. Take it in turns to pick up two jelly babies and say which two people or people groups you think they might stand for: two sets of people who would find it hard to sit down and eat together. Ask God for his peace and reconciliation. Eat the jelly babies (a non-significant action).

8

Worship

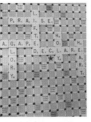

> Now while Jesus was at Bethany in the house of Simon the leper, a woman came to him with an alabaster jar of very costly ointment, and she poured it on his head as he sat at the table. But when the disciples saw it, they were angry and said, 'Why this waste? For this ointment could have been sold for a large sum, and the money given to the poor.' But Jesus, aware of this, said to them, 'Why do you trouble the woman? She has performed a good service for me. For you always have the poor with you, but you will not always have me. By pouring this ointment on my body she has prepared me for burial. Truly I tell you, wherever this good news is proclaimed in the whole world, what she has done will be told in remembrance of her.'
>
> MATTHEW 26:6–13

#discipleship

Messy team theme

- What's your favourite way to worship God?
- What do you learn about worship from worshipping with people of different ages?
- Would you say your Messy Church helps people meet God or tells them about God?

How does this session help people grow in Christ?

Perhaps some people (including some team members) think of Messy Church as a bit of fun, but have never thought of it as a way of making space for people to worship God together. This session helps us all think about worship through the worshipful, extravagant action of the woman who anointed Jesus with perfume.

Mealtime card

- What's the best scent you've ever smelled?
- Do you think the woman in today's story was wasteful or wise?
- Is church a waste of time or a wise use of time?

Take-home idea

Find out who likes worshipping where and how, in your family. Inside? Outside? At mealtime? At bedtime? By helping someone? By being noisy? Quiet? By singing? By lighting a candle? Or…? See if you can all try a very short worship experience together in each of those places or ways this month.

Question to start and end the session

So… is worship a waste?

Activities

1 Making perfume

You will need: sweet-smelling flowers and herbs, such as rose, lavender, rosemary, dandelion or blossom of any sort; water; bottles with lids; spoons; a pestle and mortar

Invite people to crush flowers and scented leaves and create a perfume of their own. Of course, this won't last more than a few hours, but is great fun to do and a very sensory activity.

Talk about how, in Jesus' time, honoured guests would be welcomed by having perfume poured over them. But on this occasion, nobody honoured Jesus, except someone very unexpected. Can only a certain type of person show they love and honour Jesus or can anyone?

2 Corner of awesomeness

You will need: items that inspire awe, such as fossils, tree bark, a photo of newborn baby or photos of space; a chalkboard and chalk or a whiteboard and pens (with the word 'Wow' written on)

Invite people to say which object they think is most awesome and whether it is just awesome on its own or makes them want to say anything to God. Draw or write any words of worship on the board.

Talk about the psalmist's words in Psalm 8 (have copies of it on the table if you can). When he saw wonderful things in nature, he turned that wonder into worship of the God who made them.

3 Scrabble worship words

You will need: a Scrabble board and tiles; a Bible

Invite people to fill up the board with interlocking worship words: words that people through the ages have used to worship God. People might even know worship words from other languages to use. If you get stuck, open the Bible at the book of Psalms and see if you can find any words there.

Talk about whether you worship God with words or actions or thoughts or...?

4 Big kiss

You will need: a large cardboard X; old magazines or collage papers; scissors; glue (alternatively, you could use a papier mâché alphabet letter X box from craft stores)

Decorate the big kiss with the collage papers.

Talk about how the English word 'worship' comes from a word that means 'come close to kiss'. The woman in today's story loved Jesus so much she wanted to be close enough to kiss him. Do you find that surprising? Weird? Beautiful? Embarrassing? How did Jesus find it?

5 Number-one God

You will need: a stamper of the numeral 1; ink pads or sponges soaked in paint; one large sheet of pictures (download online)

Invite people to think about which parts of their life they are happy for God to be in charge of – to be number one. As an act of worship, stamp one or more 1s over the picture corresponding to that part of life.

Talk about what it actually means to put God first in these areas of life.

6 Bubbling-over contest

You will need: water; fruit juice; paper straws; small beakers (shot glass-size is fine) ; bowls

Give each person a beaker, a bowl and a straw. Place the beaker in the bowl. Fill the beaker with a mix of fruit juice and water (in a bid to avoid sugary drinks but still taste nice). Challenge the group to see who can be the fastest to empty their beaker by blowing through the straw and making the liquid overflow into the bowl. Then they can drink it up. (You could even have a 'loudest slurping/sucking noise' contest to finish up with.)

Talk about the way the beaker overflowed with the drink: the liquid just couldn't stay in the beaker. That's just like the woman in the story – her love for Jesus overflowed out of her in worship. Some people thought it was a bit noisy and embarrassing and over the top – maybe inappropriate. But what did Jesus think?

7 Snuffboxes

You will need: boxes or other containers with something pleasantly strongly scented in each, such as lavender, lemon, orange, spices, herbs, roses or fresh bread (just be careful not to be so strongly scented that you induce allergic reactions)

Invite people to guess what's in each container by using their sense of smell.

Talk about what senses we use when we worship God. Which senses could we use? The woman in today's story worshipped Jesus by pouring perfume over him, releasing a wonderful smell that must have filled the whole room. In what way might we say worship is like a lovely smell?

8 Pointless?

You will need: olive oil; a jug; a bowl; towels

Pour some olive oil from the jug over someone's hands so that it drips into the bowl. Be more extravagant than you might want to be! Let the person feel the over-the-top-ness of the action. Explain how pouring oil over a guest's head, hands or feet was a way of pouring out welcome to them. It was also a way of anointing them for a special job, such as being a king or a priest. It was used to prepare someone for dying. It was used in worship, to symbolise pouring out your whole self to God.

Talk about whether this activity is a waste of good olive oil. Talk about how worship itself might seem to be pointless and a waste (of time, energy, gifts, money, etc.) to someone who doesn't know Jesus. The woman in the story was criticised for wasting the perfume. What did Jesus say? What do you think about worship? What else might seem at first to be pointless but might actually be something that is vital to being a human living well?

9 Lava lamp

> **You will need: bottles; water; vegetable oil; food colouring; fizzing tablets such as Alka-Seltzer or effervescent vitamin C tablets (use under supervision)**

Fill the bottles half full of water and colour it with the food colouring. Top the bottle up with oil. Put the lid on the bottle, give it a good shake and then watch the oil globules moving to the surface. For younger people, this may be enough (and will avoid the danger that they might drink the liquid with an Alka-Seltzer tablets in it). The coloured water can also be made to travel up through the oil and then drop down again – just like a real lava lamp. When the liquids are separated, drop in a tablet and watch the bubbles take water up through the oil.

Talk about how you can 'waste a moment' giving yourself to Jesus in the time it takes for the movement in the bottle to stop. Is it a waste of time? Or are you giving Jesus something precious to you, just as the woman in the story did?

10 Ways we worship

> **You will need: photos of different ways Christians worship, such as a modern praise service, a traditional service, people outside (perhaps taking part in something like Forest Church or just worshipping through nature), people in a Messy Church, the**

wise men before Jesus, people working in a food bank, children worshipping, Christians from other countries worshipping, your own Sunday church worshipping, someone at school, someone doing housework, someone working in a lab, factory, hospital or office; a picture of the woman in today's story worshipping Jesus; stickers (optional)

Spread out the pictures and ask people what word goes with all these pictures. Or provide stickers and invite people to put a sticker on the back of any picture they think goes with the word 'worship'. Or ask people to put the pictures in order of which is most about worship down to which is least about worship.

Talk about the choices that people have made about what is and isn't worship, especially the pictures that are, perhaps, less obviously corporate Christian worship: are they worship? How are they worship? What is worship all about?

Celebration

As long as you don't have anyone who will be adversely affected by scents (they can affect people's breathing), pour out something very strongly scented and ask people to sit very still and put their hand up when they smell it. You might want to use an essential oil on an oil burner. If you have a very large group, you could either have several scent stations scattered around the congregation or invite a sample group of people to sit at the front near the scent and do it as a demonstration to everyone else.

How interesting – some people smelled it almost straight away, some took longer and some never smelled it at all. The smell has spread around the room with no noise and is totally invisible. It's definitely there, but you can't see it or touch it.

It was a few days before Jesus died. The room in Simon's house was full of important men. It smelled a bit fusty and close, to be honest: the men had taken off their sandals, nobody had had a bath recently and there were lots of smells of the meal they'd just eaten – spices and vegetables and hot sauces – just hanging in the air.

But suddenly, in came a woman. Nobody even knew her name. She was carrying a beautiful carved alabaster jar. She went straight to Jesus as if she just had to be close to him. And she broke open the jar and poured the contents gently over his head. It was full of the most beautifully perfumed oil – the most expensive, the most delicious, the most fragrant smell you've ever smelled. The perfume spread around the room, cutting through all the fusty smells of the meal and the bodies and making everyone breathe in deeply to enjoy it to the full. She poured it all out, every last drop, the most precious thing she owned. She poured it all out for Jesus.

Some people were angry with the woman for wasting this very costly perfume on Jesus, when it could have been sold and the money given to the poor. But Jesus said, 'She has done a beautiful thing for me.'

We worship Jesus, too. How do we worship him? (*Songs, prayers, actions, service to others are just a few answers you might get.*) Some people never worship Jesus. Perhaps they've never thought of it or perhaps they think, like the people in the story, that it's a waste. It's like the perfume. But remember what Jesus thought of the woman who poured out the perfume.

I wonder how many of us take the most precious thing in our life – something we've been hoarding up for ourselves - and pour it out for Jesus, like the woman poured out her perfume. Maybe that precious thing is time. Maybe it's money. Maybe it's love. Maybe it's ourselves. We bring our best to Jesus and hand it over to him, not because we're paying him or bribing him, but because we love him and want to show our love to him. We call this worship. To some people, it looks like a waste of time and effort. But to Jesus, it's something very beautiful.

Prayer

Have one full and one empty bowl at the front and a table on which to put used cups. Give everyone an empty cup. Say the water in the bowl is a symbol for what we want to offer Jesus in worship. Invite everyone to come and fill up their cup then pour it into the empty bowl. Explain that if they would like to offer the whole of themselves to Jesus, they could pour out the whole cup of water. If they're not sure they want to do that yet, they might pour out a little bit. If they would rather not pour any out, they could either drink it or put the cup of water on the table with the others. Nobody is watching how much they pour out: it's just between them and Jesus. Play a quiet song while this is happening.

Song suggestions

- 'Music maker' – Fischy Music
- '10,000 reasons' – Matt Redman, Jonas Myrin
- 'Shout to the Lord' – Darlene Zschech

Meal suggestion

Pasta, tomato sauce, grated cheese and chopped lettuce

Messy Extra

Acts 16:25–34: Paul and Silas in prison

Read the story together.

- What do you find most interesting?
- What word or phrase stands out for you?
- Why do you think Paul and Silas were worshipping God when they'd been unjustly thrown into a horrible place? It wasn't fair!
- Who do you know or know of who keeps on worshipping God even though they're in a hard place or things are going wrong?
- What difference will this story make this week in the way you choose to worship Jesus?

Activity

Who can make the most 'musical' musical instrument from the contents of their kitchen or a stash of junk? See if you can together play a worship song on them.

Prayer

Do an internet search for 'Christian unjustly imprisoned' and find a story suitable for your group to look at together. Pray for the person or people involved.

9

Prayer

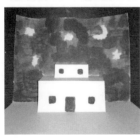

Our Father
Who art in heaven
Hallowed be thy name
Thy kingdom come
Thy will be done

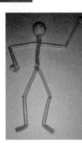

[Jesus] was praying in a certain place, and after he had finished, one of his disciples said to him, 'Lord, teach us to pray, as John taught his disciples.' He said to them, 'When you pray, say: Father, hallowed be your name. Your kingdom come. Give us each day our daily bread. And forgive us our sins, for we ourselves forgive everyone indebted to us. And do not bring us to the time of trial.'

And he said to them, 'Suppose one of you has a friend, and you go to him at midnight and say to him, "Friend, lend me three loaves of bread; for a friend of mine has arrived, and I have nothing to set before him." And he answers from within, "Do not bother me; the door has already been locked, and my children are with me in bed; I cannot get up and give you anything." I tell you, even though he will not get up and give him anything because he is his friend, at least because of his persistence he will get up and give him whatever he needs.

'So I say to you, Ask, and it will be given to you; search, and you will find; knock, and the door will be opened for you. For everyone who asks receives, and everyone who searches finds, and for everyone who knocks, the door will be opened. Is there anyone among you who, if your child asks for a fish, will give a snake instead of a fish? Or if the child asks for an egg, will give a scorpion?'

LUKE 11:1–12

#discipleship

Messy team theme

- How do we pray for our Messy Church?
- Could we pray for other Messy Churches locally and nationally?
- Who do we think is the most prayerful person in our team?

How does this session help people grow in Christ?

Listening to God and talking to God on our own, in families and as a church is one of the most basic faith-growing habits to encourage in each other. The more we pray, the more resilient our faith is in the ups and downs of life and the more we see the world through Jesus' eyes and with his compassion. Helping people of all ages to develop the habit of prayerfulness is essential to long-term discipleship.

Mealtime card

- What makes you pray?
- Where do you find it easy to pray?
- What's your favourite prayer?

Take-home idea

Choose a time of day that suits your family and make up a prayer together that you can say every day at that time. It could be bedtime or breakfast time or just before you turn on the TV. Try to pray it for this month.

Question to start and end the session

So… how do Christians pray?

Activities

1 Chalk rockets

You will need: vinegar; film canisters or other small pots with lids; cornflour; food colouring; bicarbonate of soda; a large sheet of paper; safety goggles

Spread paper over an outdoor surface like a patio. Put 1/2 tablespoon of vinegar into a canister with 1/2 tablespoon of cornflour. Add a few drops of food colouring and stir well. Put on safety goggles. Add a teaspoon of bicarbonate of soda, put the lid on the canister, turn it upside down and stand back. It should explode, leaving a coloured chalky splodge on your paper. Repeat with lots of different colours until you have a fine, if soggy, piece of art.

Talk about the colourfulness your chalk rockets brought to the dull paper. Prayer brings colour into dull or dark situations; it's a way of shining Jesus' light and hope into somewhere that needs it.

2 Scratch art

You will need: wax crayons; pieces of card; black poster paint; liquid soap; paint brushes; scratching sticks (cocktail sticks or wooden skewers)

You can prepare these in advance or let the families make them on the day, but that will mean allowing drying time. I suggest having a few ready-made and some to create from scratch (haha). Colour all over the card until it's covered with different colours. Paint over the colour with black paint into which you have mixed a little liquid soap. Leave to dry. Scrape off the black in designs.

Talk about the way that praying about something is a bit like scraping off the surface to reveal what's really there. That's why Jesus told his friends 'seek and you will find'. One way to seek God's way of doing things is to keep on praying about it until he shows you.

3 Confetti egg

You will need: eggshells, as intact as possible; tissue paper in lots of bright colours; scissors; glue; a few prepared eggs already sealed as below (as a less messy and more eco-friendly alternative, you could fill the eggs with birdseed and crack them outside)

Cut up your two favourite colours of tissue paper into tiny pieces of confetti and fill your egg loosely with them. Glue tissue paper over the hole in the eggshell, then decorate the outside of the egg with coloured tissue paper.

Gather a group together with their (dry) eggs and one of your prepared ones. Say that Jesus wanted his friends to know that God loves to give his people GOOD answers to prayer, and he isn't a God of nasty surprises. He said that if you asked your dad for an egg, would he give you a scorpion as a nasty joke? No, of course not! (You may need to be sensitive to situations of abuse here.) We've got eggs full of happy confetti here: but what is MY EGG full of? Something nasty or something nice? How much do you trust me? Let's ask permission from someone else and crack our eggs open on their head to see what's inside… All the eggs are fine!

Talk about how God never plays nasty jokes on us.

4 Decorated teaspoons

You will need: teaspoons; nail varnish or glass paints; tiny brushes; marker pens

Decorate a teaspoon to remind you to pray: the abbreviation for teaspoon, TSP, can also stand for Thank you, Sorry, Please – three sorts of prayers to pray.

Talk about how saying 'thank you' to God for good things around us is a really good habit, especially when we don't feel like giving thanks. Saying 'sorry' is good for us because it helps free us from horrible guilty feelings. And saying 'please' is an invitation to ask God to help people we love and places we care about.

5 Bottle top spinner

You will need: a plastic lid from a bottle; a wooden skewer; thick card; pens; stick-on gems; scissors; a bradawl; a screwdriver

Make a hole in the centre of the bottle cap using the sharp tools. Cut out a hexagon from the card, slightly larger than the bottle cap. Write along each edge of the hexagon a different way to pray or person/place to pray for (e.g. Thank you; Wow; You are…; Family; Country; School or work). Decorate the hexagon with a simple pattern or the stick-on gems. Stick the skewer through the centre of the card, then through the plastic lid from the top to the bottom and have about 1 cm extra of the pointy end sticking out below the edge of the lid. Trim the skewer to about 15 cm or a comfortable length to twirl. Colour the stick if you want to. Twirl the spinning top and see what sort of prayer it lands on. Pray the prayer.

Talk about the different ways of praying that you enjoy.

6 Ring and the door shall be opened

You will need: egg cartons; scissors; paint; paint brushes; jingle bells; chunky beads; thread or wool; a darning needle

Cut the egg cradles off the egg carton so they are single cups. Paint them and allow to dry. Thread a needle with wool and tie a big knot in the end. Catch the jingle bell on to the wool, followed by one or two beads, then thread through the base of the egg cradle from the inside, so you have the jingle bell and beads making the clapper of the bell. Leave a length of wool to tie the bells up with. Make several and hang them from your door handle at home. You could make a little sign saying 'Please ring'.

Talk about Jesus' words 'knock and the door will be opened to you' – it's as if he's waiting behind the door for you to call on him. When you 'knock on the door' with your prayer, he just wants to open up the door and welcome you!

7 Pop-up house

You will need: lightweight card; scissors; pencils; paints; paint brushes

Tell the story of the friend at midnight from Luke 11: now you're going to make a dark sleepy house at midnight.

Fold the card in half across the width. Cut two parallel slits through both thicknesses across the fold: these form the walls and flat roof of the house. Open up the card and reverse the folds so the house stands out. (You can repeat as many times as you like to build storeys on top of each other – just let people experiment.) Flatten it out and paint on the dark windows and doors and a dark sky with moon and stars in the background. When it's dry, stand it up again.

It's a very simple activity so some people might want to make another one - the 'after' house: the same house but all lit up after the friend has arrived, with wailing babies and faces at the windows!

Talk about the way Jesus encourages us to bring everything to God in prayer, even if it seems – like the friend at midnight – to be an unreasonable request! God loves us and wants to help us.

8 Eggciting eggs

You will need: hard-boiled eggs; a knife; a chopping board; an icing bag and nozzle or a plastic bag with the corner cut off; a bowl; a fork; a spoon; salt; paper; mayonnaise; mustard; curry powder; paprika (alternative for vegans/people allergic to egg: melon slice with filling of yoghurt and berries)

(Check for allergies.) Peel the eggs and cut them in half. Separate the whites and the yolks. Put the whites to one side. Mix the yolks in a bowl with the other ingredients (or as many as the families want to use). Place the mixture in the icing bag and squeeze attractively into the egg whites. Sprinkle with paprika if required.

Talk about what Jesus says in Luke 11 about God wanting to give his children good things, just like a dad who wants to give his hungry child a delicious egg and won't shock them by giving them a scorpion instead.

9 Calligraphy

You will need: calligraphy pens and inks; lined paper; alphabets to copy (find in books or online)

Give people a chance to draw the Lord's Prayer in calligraphy.

Talk about how sometimes taking longer to write something down and taking care over each letter can help us to relax and come more easily into God's presence. How might you prepare to meet God through mindfulness or meditation?

10 Prayer action heroes

You will need: pipe cleaners; drinking straws; scissors; big beads; marker pens

Make a person shape out of two or three pipe cleaners, then cut straws into smaller pieces and use them to form the limbs of the figure, to give it more substance and make it easier to pose. Use the bead as the head and draw on a face. Your very own prayer action hero!

Talk about how prayer can be actions as well as words. Can you show some different ways your figure might use its body to pray? Hands together, kneeling or…?

Celebration

Put a chair out in the middle of your gathering and declare that it's the 'Chair of Prayer'.

Today we've been thinking about one of the ways we grow closer to Jesus and that's by praying.

Invite someone to come and sit on the chair and share one thing they know about prayer, perhaps something they've learned today. Repeat this a few times with different people and lots of applause.

Then invite someone (probably pre-arranged and from the team) to sit on the chair and share their favourite prayer and why they like it and when they say it.

Invite a parent and child to share their bedtime prayer habit or what they pray before meals.

Invite someone (probably pre-arranged and from the team) to sit on the chair and share a time when they prayed and nothing seemed to happen but they kept on praying.

Repeat with someone who prayed and something changed more obviously.

We're trying to follow Jesus, so we want to do the things he and his friends did.

In today's story, Jesus prayed to God, and his disciples wanted to pray like he did. So Jesus taught them a special prayer, which Christians all over the world now pray. You don't have to be in a special place like the Chair of Prayer or in a church building to pray: you can pray anywhere at any time.

And it's much easier to talk about prayer than to get on and pray! So let's pray now…

Prayer

Pray the Lord's Prayer with actions (messychurch.org.uk/resource/lords-prayer-actions) or use the version from the end of *The Lord's Prayer Unplugged* (BRF, 2012).

Song suggestions

- 'Build your kingdom here' – Rend Collective
- 'Bring it all to me' – Fischy Music
- 'Big big questions' – Fischy Music

Meal suggestion

Egg sandwiches (to go with the egg/scorpion theme), or chilli in a hollowed-out bread bun (to go with the friend at midnight).

Messy Extra

Acts 27: Paul is shipwrecked

Read the story together.

- Have you ever been in a situation anything like this?
- What do you find most puzzling?
- What do you find most interesting?
- What word or phrase stands out for you?
- What do you think of Paul's prayer?
- What difference will this story make this week in your walk with Jesus?

Activity

Make origami boats.

Prayer

As you place your origami boats on the surface of a bowl of water. Pray for someone going through a dangerous or scary time.

10

Breaking Bread

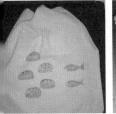

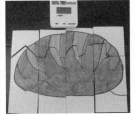

After these things Jesus showed himself again to the disciples by the Sea of Tiberias; and he showed himself in this way. Gathered there together were Simon Peter, Thomas called the Twin, Nathanael of Cana in Galilee, the sons of Zebedee, and two others of his disciples. Simon Peter said to them, 'I am going fishing.' They said to him, 'We will go with you.' They went out and got into the boat, but that night they caught nothing.

Just after daybreak, Jesus stood on the beach; but the disciples did not know that it was Jesus. Jesus said to them, 'Children, you have no fish, have you?' They answered him, 'No.' He said to them, 'Cast the net to the right side of the boat, and you will find some.' So they cast it, and now they were not able to haul it in because there were so many fish. That disciple whom Jesus loved said to Peter, 'It is the Lord!' When Simon Peter heard that it was the Lord, he put on some clothes, for he was naked, and jumped into the lake. But the other disciples came in the boat, dragging the net full of fish, for they were not far from the land, only about a hundred yards off.

When they had gone ashore, they saw a charcoal fire there, with fish on it, and bread. Jesus said to them, 'Bring some of the fish that you have just caught.' So Simon Peter went aboard and hauled the net ashore, full of large fish, a hundred and fifty-three of them; and though there were so many, the net was not torn. Jesus said to them, 'Come and have breakfast.' Now none of the disciples dared to ask him, 'Who are you?' because they knew it was the Lord. Jesus came and took the bread and gave it to them, and did the same with the fish. This was now the third time that Jesus appeared to the disciples after he was raised from the dead.

JOHN 21:1–14

#discipleship

Messy team theme

- What does Holy Communion mean to you?
- When was the last time you broke bread with someone not from your own home?
- What needs breaking and re-forming in your church?

How does this session help people grow in Christ?

Nobody is 100% certain whether the reference to the first followers of Jesus 'breaking bread together' means that they ate meals together or intentionally remembered Jesus' death and resurrection by breaking bread together. In a form of church like Messy Church, where a meal is built into the 'liturgy' every time, and where it may be more helpful to enrich the understanding around simply being at a table together (rather than getting tied up in knots about who can take Communion and who can't), we are in the privileged position of not needing to worry about the discrepancy. Whether it's the warmth of fellowship around a meal table or the warmth of fellowship around a Communion table, breaking bread as a holy habit can draw people together as a family and can remind us all of Jesus' death and resurrection.

Mealtime card

- What's the most amazing thing for you about your tummy and how it works?
- Have you ever broken something really precious?
- Why do you think Jesus gave his friends a meal to remember him by?

Take-home idea

Why not have a picnic together and, as you share the sandwiches round in the beautiful park, wood or seaside, tell each other one of the stories of Jesus sharing bread with his friends?

Question to start and end the session

So… what gets even better when you break it?

Activities

Note on allergies
Be aware that some participants may have a gluten allergy. Consider planning alternatives to activities that involve real bread/dough.

1 Breakfast in a jar

> **You will need: oats; nuts (beware allergies); dried fruits; granola; small clean jars with lids; spoons; twine; luggage labels**

Make a breakfast in a jar – just add milk and eat! Spoon layers of ingredients into the jar, trying to leave them in clearly defined strata until the jar is packed full. Put on the lid and write a label to tie on with twine

Talk about what you eat for breakfast. Jesus cooked his friends fish and bread after they'd had a hard night at sea. This was after he had come back from the dead. They sat and ate breakfast together on the beach. Who could you share your breakfast jar with?

2 Hovercraft

> **You will need: old CDs (or you could use any similar-sized piece of light card or plastic tray to experiment with); sports bottle tops; balloons; glue guns**

Glue the bottle top on to the CD over the hole in the centre. Attach an inflated balloon on to the bottle top. Watch it hover!

Talk about how Peter had a boat not a hovercraft (but no doubt would have loved driving a hovercraft). He'd seen Jesus dead and alive again, but Jesus wasn't with him all the time. As his boat came close to shore, he recognised Jesus on the beach. What do you think Peter did then?

3 Campfire cooking

You will need: prepared bread dough (risen or not); long, clean sticks; a campfire or firepit

Cook 'dampers' over the fire's embers: a twist of dough around the end of a stick. (You might like to let a Scouter or someone in a similar role organise this activity, who knows how to do it safely.)

Talk about how Jesus cooked bread and fish for his friends for breakfast after he rose from the dead. Why do you think he wanted to eat with them?

4 Prayer clock

You will need: paper plates; card; scissors; pens; split pins; food catalogues or photos of different sorts of bread

Make a 'prayer clock' to let the times you eat bread remind you to pray. Put a picture of the sort of bread you eat at the right time on the clock face – for example, a piece of toast at 7.00 am, a sandwich at 12.00 noon, a burger bun at 5.00 pm. In the centre write: 'Give us today our daily bread.'

Talk about how, for people who follow Jesus, the special meal of bread and wine reminds them of Jesus' death and resurrection.

5 Tearing bread

You will need: bread dough; flavourings (such as rosemary sprigs, crushed garlic or dried herbs); baking trays; an oven

Make a miniature version of a tearing loaf. Take a piece of the prepared dough and form it into four small balls. Roll in the flavouring. Place them close enough together on the baking tray that, as they go through their final proving, they will clump together to make one small loaf. Bake when it has risen, then tear and share.

Talk about how the act of taking a whole piece of bread and dividing it between people is laden with symbolism. It is only by breaking the bread that it can be shared out: how does that help us understand Jesus' body 'broken for us' on the cross?

6 Bread in art

You will need: a laptop and access to YouTube; loaves of white sliced bread

Invite people to watch the four-minute YouTube Tateshots video of the sculptor Antony Gormley talking about his artwork using bread (search for 'Antony Gormley Breaking Bread'). As you watch the video, let people handle the slices of bread and play with them as Gormley does and eat them if they want to.

Talk about what you think of what he says. How do you feel about using food in art? Do you remember what he says about breaking bread for his bed sculpture? Does this help you see Holy Communion in a different light?

7 Bread bag

You will need: cotton drawstring bags (surprisingly cheap online – under £1 each); fabric pens, paints or marker pens; children's Bibles with pictures

Think of your favourite Bible story about bread. Decorate a bag with an illustration of that story and use it as a bread bag for a home-made loaf.

Talk about the way Jesus broke bread with his friends in many ways – sometimes in a crowd, sometimes in a very small group of friends. Which story of bread is the most important, in your opinion? Why?

8 A cone of breadsticks

You will need: breadsticks; melted chocolate in a bowl; a bowl of warm water; sprinkles; greaseproof paper; clean paper; means of drawing a circle (a template or compasses); scissors; coloured pens; sticky tape

Break your breadsticks in half. Dip the rounded end in the melted chocolate then coat with sprinkles. (Keep the melted chocolate over a bowl of warm water and do a good risk assessment to minimise the risk of spillage.) Place the breadsticks on greaseproof paper and allow them to set.

Meanwhile, make a paper cone by cutting a circle out of paper, then cutting a small segment out of the circle, decorating the circle with a pattern, shaping it into a cone and taping it together. Put your breadsticks into the cone and share them with others.

Talk about how it feels to keep things to yourself. How does it feel to share them around? What did Jesus show his friends about sharing, using bread?

9 Break and make challenge

You will need: a homemade jigsaw – a picture of bread drawn on card and cut up into 8–10 pieces; a timer

Invite teams of three or more to participate together against the clock. Make up the jigsaw so the 'whole' picture can be seen. Then shuffle all the pieces and distribute them to the team members. Can they bring the pieces together and reassemble the jigsaw more quickly than other teams? Keep a note of the teams and their timings.

Talk about the way the bread was whole, then broken up, then put back together again. When God's people break bread together, especially at Communion, the bread gets broken and shared out among lots of people. In what way do you think that bread gets 'put back together again'? (You might like to think what the bread stands for.)

10 Breaking good

You will need: plates; pieces of different types of bread, such as sliced, pitta, poppadom and flatbread (alternatively, use pictures of bread and scissors)

Invite people to break the bread up and reassemble the pieces on the plate as something different. Then eat the resultant picture or sculpture (unless you've done the paper version).

Talk about how different the finished picture is from the original piece of bread. It's the same material but it's been transformed by your imagination and creativity. Breaking bread, either at a meal eaten together or at Communion, does something similar. A very ordinary, everyday object is transformed by God's creativity into something different. What changes do you see when people break bread together? When your Messy Church breaks bread together?

Celebration

It was just after Jesus rose from the dead and his friends were confused. Happy, but confused. They just weren't expecting Jesus to die or to come back from the dead, and it took a bit of getting used to. Everything was different. Everything had changed. It was exciting. But it wasn't comfy. So Peter and the others went out on the lake to do a bit of fishing. Fishing is calming and normal if you're a fisherman. But they fished all night and didn't catch anything!

When it got to morning and they were close to the shore again, someone called to them from the beach. 'Have you caught anything?' shouted a voice. 'No!' they all shouted back, rather grumpily. 'Throw your nets out on the other side of the boat!' shouted the voice. And when they did, straight away the nets filled up with over 100 fish! Peter remembered a time three years ago when something very much the same had happened in his boat, and he knew who the stranger on the beach was. He jumped into the water (yes – with all his clothes on!) and splashed his way to the beach, where the stranger was waiting. And yes! It was Jesus!

Jesus wasn't busy painting sunrises or creating galaxies that day. He was simply cooking bread for breakfast. So they brought some of the fish they had just caught as well and Jesus added them to the meal. Jesus broke the bread up and gave it, and the fish, to his friends, and they had the best picnic breakfast ever. The stranger shared his bread and was a friend. In the middle of so much extraordinariness, Jesus did something very, very ordinary. He made bread and shared it out. Perhaps Peter and the disciples remembered the other times Jesus had broken bread with them. Do you remember any of those times?

Breaking bread together is something we can all do, from the youngest person to the oldest person, and from the person who doesn't know Jesus yet to the person who is already following him. When we break bread together at Communion or at our meal table, let's always remember Jesus is there with us, turning strangers into friends, putting the broken back together again in a new and unexpected way.

Prayer

Pass round a (gluten-free if necessary) bread roll and invite everyone to think about the way it's broken up between so many people. You might want to use one of the Messy Communion services from messychurch.org.uk/holy-communion. Now we all have a piece of the same bread inside us.

Song suggestions

- 'As we are gathered, Jesus is here' – Authentic Publishing
- 'As we go now' – Fischy Music
- 'When people are cruel' – Fischy Music

Meal suggestion

Anything involving bread, such as pizza, wraps or sandwiches

Messy Extra

1 Corinthians 11:17–26:
The Jesus-followers make a mess

Read the story together.

- What do you find most interesting?
- What word or phrase stands out for you?
- Why do you think Paul was so bothered by the way these Jesus-followers were breaking bread together?
- How can we be 'different' from each other but not 'divided'?
- Talk about how you all find breaking bread in your church.
- What difference will this story make this week in your walk with Jesus?

Activity

Make bread rolls together and make one extra to use in the prayer.

Prayer

Read out 1 Corinthians 11:23–24 and pass round the bread roll, each tearing off a piece and saving it until everyone has got a piece before you eat it.

11

Fellowship

[Jesus said,] 'I am the true vine, and my Father is the vine-grower. He removes every branch in me that bears no fruit. Every branch that bears fruit he prunes to make it bear more fruit. You have already been cleansed by the word that I have spoken to you. Abide in me as I abide in you. Just as the branch cannot bear fruit by itself unless it abides in the vine, neither can you unless you abide in me. I am the vine, you are the branches. Those who abide in me and I in them bear much fruit, because apart from me you can do nothing. Whoever does not abide in me is thrown away like a branch and withers; such branches are gathered, thrown into the fire, and burned. If you abide in me, and my words abide in you, ask for whatever you wish, and it will be done for you. My Father is glorified by this, that you bear much fruit and become my disciples. As the Father has loved me, so I have loved you; abide in my love. If you keep my commandments, you will abide in my love, just as I have kept my Father's commandments and abide in his love. I have said these things to you so that my joy may be in you, and that your joy may be complete.

'This is my commandment, that you love one another as I have loved you. No one has greater love than this, to lay down one's life for one's friends. You are my friends if you do what I command you. I do not call you servants any longer, because the servant does not know what the master is doing; but I have called you friends, because I have made known to you everything that I have heard from my Father. You did not choose me but I chose you. And I appointed you to go and bear fruit, fruit that will last, so that the Father will give you whatever you ask him in my name. I am giving you these commands so that you may love one another.'

JOHN 15:1–17

#discipleship

Messy team theme

- What's the difference between friendship and fellowship?
- Take a moment to review your connectedness: are all your contact details and lists up to date?
- What do you value most about the fellowship of your Messy Church team?

How does this session help people grow in Christ?

There's something about fellowship that means we are all connected, needed and, though different, equally valued; we are not alone. Fellowship is the practice that helps us as a church or as church groups to look outwards and welcome absolutely everyone, whoever they are. In communities where loneliness and isolation are problems, the fellowship of a church may be a lifeline.

Mealtime card

- What's the best thing about your best friend?
- Have you ever done a 'friendly' thing for someone who wasn't your friend?
- What do you think 'the fellowship of the Holy Spirit' is like?

Take-home idea

Think about someone you haven't seen in church for a while. Why not take them a bunch of grapes with a card that has John 15:5a on to show you're thinking of them and miss them?

Question to start and end the session

So… can't we be Christians all on our own?

Activities

1 Washi tape

You will need: printable sticker paper; a pencil; a ruler; felt-tip pens or paints and brushes; a craft knife or guillotine

Make your own washi tape. You might want to do a grapevine design to echo the theme of the day. If using felt-tip pens, first cut the paper into long, straight strips about 5 mm wide using a craft knife, then invite people to decorate them. If using paint, paint the colours you like in narrow stripes across the whole sheet of paper, leaving no white spaces. Allow the paint to dry, then slice the paper up with a craft knife or guillotine into 5 mm strips. The tape can be used at home to decorate stationery or other similar items.

Talk about sticking things together and the different ways we can stick objects together. What sticks people together and holds them together? Jesus says we all need to be stuck to him like branches, which are so stuck to a vine they are actually part of it! That's sticky!

2 Magnetic attraction

You will need: paperclips; bar magnets; light card cutouts of people (about 5 cm tall); a blindfold

Attach a paperclip to each cut-out person. Spread them out across the tabletop. Blindfold someone and give them a bar magnet to hold in one hand. Their challenge is to pick up as many people with the magnet as they can in one minute using only the magnet and not their other hand.

Talk about the way the people get stuck together by the magnetic force attracting the steel paperclips. As they get pulled towards the magnet, they get pulled towards each other. In churches, as people who are very, very different from each other get pulled towards Jesus by his love, we also get pulled towards each other. We call this fellowship.

3 Ivy planters

You will need: plastic milk bottles in a range of sizes with lids; scissors; marker pens; compost; rooted ivy cuttings

In colder climates, it's hard to grow grapevines, but we can grow another sort of vine – ivy. Design your own planter for your ivy! Think about which way up is best for your planter. Will it stand on a shelf or hang from a hook on a wall? Do you want it plain or decorated to look like a face, an animal, a vehicle, a monster…? Can you see the start of a design like that in any part of the milk bottle?

Use the marker pens to mark where you will cut plastic away and to make any decorative markings on it. Cut it to shape and fill with compost and plant an ivy plant.

Talk about how our ivy won't bear fruit like a grapevine. Why do you think Jesus talked about his friends and himself being like branches of a grapevine? How can we stay as close to Jesus as branches to a vine?

4 Big picture

You will need: long rolls of paper such as lining paper; paint; rollers; round sponges

Go big! Encourage everyone to take the rollers and roll out paint to make the trunk and branches of the vine. This vine is HUGE! Then add leaves (handprints?) and grapes (round sponge prints or thumbprints).

Talk about what would happen if a branch was cut off. How many leaves would it have? How much fruit? Jesus wanted his friends to live in fellowship with him and with each other, all connected like branches to a vine, so we would produce lots of fruit. What sort of fruit comes from families or churches where people are close to each other and trust each other?

5 Paper quilt

You will need: strips of patterned paper about 2 cm wide; scissors; glue; backing paper; print-offs of 'log cabin quilt' designs

If you have a quilter in your church, it would be lovely to make a real quilt together, as quilts have always been a way for people to connect over a shared project. But most of us don't, so it's paper and glue!

Invite people to create their own paper log cabin quilt design by cutting paper strips to the right length and gluing them together carefully.

Talk about how quilts join up lots of scraps of fabric that otherwise would have been thrown away. How is that like the church? How do we make strong connections between us and God at the centre and between each other?

6 Together we're brighter!

You will need: lots of felt-tip pens; sticky tape; paper

Choose some pens to tape together, then try drawing with them. Adjust the angle until they're comfortable. Add more pens. Have fun designing with your super-pen.

Talk about the joys and frustrations of having your pens connected together. What are the joys and frustrations of being connected to others in the church?

7 Grape sculpture

You will need: cocktail sticks; grapes; raisins; plates

Allocate a number of grapes and raisins to each person, together with a stack of cocktail sticks, and invite them to create a sculpture on the theme of 'Connected'.

Talk about Jesus' image of the branches needing to be connected to the vine if they are to be fruitful. What helps people to be connected to Jesus?

8 Foil initial

You will need: kitchen foil; corrugated cardboard (from old boxes); scissors; thick string; glue; marker pens

Cut out a square or rectangle of cardboard about the size of half a postcard (some people may want to make a larger one, as it's less fiddly). Cut a piece of string about 20 cm long and use the string to make your initial on the card. Glue it in place and trim off any extra string. Press a piece of foil over the top of the card, easing it into place so all the foil is touching either string or card with no foil stretched over thin air. Fold the foil into place around the back of the card. Now use marker pens in deep colours to put a grapevine design around your initial. Make a vine branch out of crumpled foil and display the initials on the branch until home time.

Talk about the way all the people here, represented by their initial, are connected together and will never be isolated or on their own: they belong together, help each other, care for each other and look out for each other. Jesus wants his church to be like that, full of different sorts of people who all connect to each other through him.

9 Very big vine

You will need: chicken wire; wire cutters; newspaper; brown, green and purple tissue, wrapping or craft paper/crêpe paper; purple balloons; string; scissors; sticky tape

Make a huge vine to fill your building. Make a trunk out of chicken wire and cover it with newspaper and then with brown paper. Use crumpled-up newspaper to form branches coming off it. Suspend the vine from beams or lay it across the back of pews. Cut out leaves of green paper and tape them on. Make grapes from bunches of purple balloons and attach.

Talk about what 'fellowship' means to everyone. What did it mean to the first Christians, when Luke says they 'devoted themselves to fellowship'?

10 Snappy painting

You will need: shallow metal trays with firm sides (such as baking trays with sides); elastic bands; sticky tape; paper; paint; paint brushes; aprons; goggles; floor coverings

This is a messy one, best done outside or well away from walls and party dresses. Put a piece of paper in the tray, tape it in place and stretch elastic bands across the tray widthways. Paint the elastic bands brown. Then snap the bands so that the paint splatters on the paper to make the suggestion of the trunk and branches of the vine. Once done, put elastic bands on lengthways and paint them green. Repeat the splattering for the leaves of the vine. Then put dollops of purple paint on to the elastic bands and splatter again for bunches of grapes.

Talk about why we love having adults as well as children at Messy Church. One reason is that we want to grow a fellowship with all sorts of different people and that means different ages, as we all have different things to learn, to give and that we need from each other.

Celebration

Stand everyone in a circle, facing inwards. In the centre of the circle, have a box with spools of wool in it, ready to be unrolled. (You may need to do a 'please don't strangle anyone' warning.)

Jesus had a big job for his disciples to do: he wanted them to change the whole planet! He wanted them to bring his kingdom of life-changing things like love, joy, peace, patience and much, much more to every part of the world. It was a huge job!

The disciples were great people. But Jesus knew that if they stayed close to him, they would be even greater, and that if they stayed in fellowship with each other, they would be greater still. And much more of the world would be changed for the better.

So before he died on the cross, he told them this:

(Have somebody read the passage slowly and, as each sentence is read, unroll a spool of wool and pass the end to someone in the circle. Gesture to them to keep holding the end but to unroll some more wool and give it to someone else in the circle. They do the same, and at the same time, you can start another spool of wool unrolling in another part of the circle, as many as you need to, with everyone ending up holding on to the wool. Read the passage through several times if you need more time to get everyone joined in.)

I am the true vine, and my Father is the gardener.
   Remain in me, as I also remain in you. No branch can bear fruit by itself; it must remain in the vine. Neither can you bear fruit unless you remain in me.
   I am the vine; you are the branches. If you remain in me and I in you, you will bear much fruit.
   If you do not remain in me, you are like a branch that is thrown away and withers.
   If you remain in me and my words remain in you, ask whatever you wish, and it will be done for you.
   You did not choose me, but I chose you and appointed you so that you might go and bear fruit – fruit that will last. This is my command: love each other.
From JOHN 15

Look at us! We're all joined to each other and we're all joined to the centre. Jesus knows we need each other to do his work in changing the world, and we need to be connected to him. We can stay connected by praying, reading our Bibles, coming to church... any other ideas?

But here's a challenge: we're all facing inwards! And if we want to change the world, we need to be looking outwards too! I wonder if we can carefully turn and face outwards without anybody dropping the vine...

Perhaps if anyone feels they'd like to be more closely connected, they could have a word and see if we could help them find a way.

Let's pray while we hold the vine.

Prayer

Loving Jesus, thank you for our Messy fellowship, where no one gets left behind. Thank you for the community around us. Help us to stay close to you and close to each other this month, so that we can make a difference in this part of the world. Help us know we are never alone, however hard our different journeys may be. Amen

Now I wonder if we can untangle this wool together!

Song suggestions

- 'Welcome everybody' – Fischy Music
- 'Build up' – Fischy Music
- 'You are a star' – Fischy Music

Meal suggestion

Spaghetti that tangles up like the wool in the celebration, tomato and bacon sauce, cheese and carrot sticks

Messy Extra

2 Corinthians 13:11–13: Living in peace with each other

Read this short passage through three times, with different voices reading.

- Why do you think Paul finished his letter with this passage?
- Which words do you think the Christians in Corinth would have found easiest to obey?
- Which would they have found most difficult?
- What has this passage got to do with Jesus' words in John 15:1–17?
- Which of Paul's words here are most important for your church or group at the moment?
- How could you put them into action this month?

Activity

Do a jigsaw together, with a focus on putting what is broken back together.

Prayer

Take a piece of paper each and write your name at the top. Pass it to the person on your left. They draw or write a prayer for that person at the bottom of the paper and fold it up so it can't be seen. Pass it on to the person on your left and repeat for the new name. Repeat until you get your paper back again.

12

Messy Vintage sessions

Messy Vintage brings 'church' to older people in care homes, in churches and in the community. Like Messy Church, Messy Vintage is Christ-centred, creative, full of celebration and hospitality, and open to all. The sessions that follow have been simplified for this specific audience.

1

The Jesus habit

> [Jesus said,] 'I am the good shepherd. The good shepherd lays down his life for the sheep. The hired hand, who is not the shepherd and does not own the sheep, sees the wolf coming and leaves the sheep and runs away – and the wolf snatches them and scatters them. The hired hand runs away because a hired hand does not care for the sheep. I am the good shepherd. I know my own and my own know me, just as the Father knows me and I know the Father. And I lay down my life for the sheep.'
>
> JOHN 10:11–15

Activity: Spot the habit

You will need: printouts of Acts 2:42–47; cards with a holy habit on each (download online)

Challenge people to find each habit in the passage: it's a description of what the first Jesus-followers did and how they followed Jesus in their everyday lives.

Talk about which habit you found most interesting? Do you think it's possible to have these habits today? Who do you know who has any of them already?

Celebration

Today we're going to think about holy habits.

What bad habits can people think of? Why is it so hard to stop once you start?

But what if *good* habits were just as hard to stop once you start? What if you just couldn't help doing holy things once you catch the habit?

The first people to follow Jesus had much harder lives than we do. If they were caught worshipping Jesus, they could be thrown in prison – even killed (as some Christians are today in some countries). The first Jesus-followers needed to help each other be strong and keep on following Jesus, even when it was hard, even when it was dangerous. And do you know what made it easier? They were *together*. They helped each other. They knew they were never alone. *Together* they prayed, read God's word and worshipped God. *Together* they served their community and were generous to each other. They had meals together and broke bread together. They even shared their possessions with each other so nobody was in need.

I wonder how we can help each other catch these holy habits and follow our good shepherd even more closely? Perhaps just being *together* today is a really good start.

Prayer

Thank God that you are all together on this adventure and ask God for help to follow Jesus more closely, like sheep following a wonderful shepherd.

Song suggestion

- 'The Lord's my shepherd' – Crimond (traditional version) or Stuart Townend

2

Gladness and Generosity

Then the son said to him, 'Father, I have sinned against heaven and before you; I am no longer worthy to be called your son.' But the father said to his slaves, 'Quickly, bring out a robe – the best one – and put it on him; put a ring on his finger and sandals on his feet. And get the fatted calf and kill it, and let us eat and celebrate; for this son of mine was dead and is alive again; he was lost and is found!' And they began to celebrate.

LUKE 15:21–24

Activity: Freely felt-tipping

You will need: black pens; other colouring pens; paper; a copy of Matthew 10:8 ('Freely you have received; freely give', NIV); a Bible

Turn Jesus' words in Matthew 10:8 into a colouring poster for a family member or friend to colour in.

Talk about whether you prefer to give or receive. What do you consider yourself to have received freely? Look at the Bible – who was Jesus talking to? What did he mean?

Celebration

You will need: plenty of pens; some small cardboard heart shapes (enough for everyone to have one)

The very first followers of Jesus decided they wanted to live their whole lives as close as they possibly could to how Jesus wanted them to be. One of the ways they lived was 'with glad and generous hearts'. What sort of a difference do you think it made to the people around them, that they had 'glad and generous hearts'?

Who do you know who has a glad and generous heart? The father in the story was glad and generous, and we can know that God is loving and generous to us.

Give everybody a cardboard cut-out of a heart and invite them to draw a smiley face on it and put it in their pocket or handbag to remind them to try to be as glad and generous as the father in the story today.

Prayer

Dear Jesus, as we put these heart shapes in a safe place, we ask for your help to make us glad and generous towards everyone we meet this week. Amen

Song suggestion

- 'Amazing grace' – John Newton

3

Making More Disciples

> Now the eleven disciples went to Galilee, to the mountain to which Jesus had directed them. When they saw him, they worshipped him; but some doubted. And Jesus came and said to them, 'All authority in heaven and on earth has been given to me. Go therefore and make disciples of all nations, baptising them in the name of the Father and of the Son and of the Holy Spirit, and teaching them to obey everything that I have commanded you. And remember, I am with you always, to the end of the age.'
>
> MATTHEW 28:16–20

Activity: Throw 'n' pray

You will need: the template of a cube (download online); coloured pens; scissors; sticky tape

Draw or write the names of five people you'd like to introduce to Jesus, one on each face of the cube. Put yourself on the final face. Cut it out, fold it and stick it together to make a die. Decide on a time each day to roll the die and pray for the person who is on the uppermost face.

Talk about the fact that, when we decide to make more disciples, we're not alone. The Holy Spirit is our helper and gives us a helping hand. The best way we can ask for help is by praying.

Celebration

We're going to see if we can spread a secret word around the room just by whispering it to two people. Surely this is impossible!

Whisper an easy word like 'picnic' to two people and tell them to whisper it to two more people. Those four people can whisper it to two people each: how long does it take before everyone in the room has heard the secret word? Can you all shout it at once? You might want to try it again with a different word to see if you can do it any faster. And yes, some people hear the word wrong and some people share the wrong word on purpose (which is quite funny all the same), so that makes it all the more important to tell not just one person, not just two people, but as many people as we can all about Jesus.

Jesus had come back from the dead, proving that he really was God. But only a tiny number of people knew that. This was God's secret to share with the whole world. Jesus gave the job of passing on the good news, not to two of his disciples but to eleven of them. Imagine if each of them had told just two people, who had told just two people, who had told just two people… I wonder if the good news about Jesus would have spread as far as us, in a very far away country thousands of years later. The way new disciples are made is by old disciples – whether you're five years old or 95 years old – sharing the good news of Jesus with people we meet. We need to share it with older people who might have been missed out and with younger people who haven't had the chance to hear it yet. Who can you share the good news about Jesus with this month?

Prayer

The best way to start sharing the good news is by asking Jesus to help us. Sit very quietly, if you can, for just a moment and ask Jesus to bring into your mind the name of one person he'd like you to pray for.

Let's pray for those people together.

Loving Jesus, thank you for the people you've put on our minds right now. Help us to be good friends to them and share the good news about you when the time is right. Amen

Song suggestion

- 'Let all the world in every corner sing' – George Herbert

4

Sharing Resources

[Jesus said,] 'The king will say to those at his right hand, "Come, you that are blessed by my Father, inherit the kingdom prepared for you from the foundation of the world; for I was hungry and you gave me food, I was thirsty and you gave me something to drink, I was a stranger and you welcomed me, I was naked and you gave me clothing, I was sick and you took care of me, I was in prison and you visited me."

Then the righteous will answer him, "Lord, when was it that we saw you hungry and gave you food, or thirsty and gave you something to drink? And when was it that we saw you a stranger and welcomed you, or naked and gave you clothing? And when was it that we saw you sick or in prison and visited you?"

And the king will answer them, "Truly I tell you, just as you did it to one of the least of these who are members of my family, you did it to me."'

MATTHEW 25:34–40

Activity: Thirsty candle

You will need: a candle; a plate; coloured water; matches; a glass that fits over the candle

Cover the plate with coloured water a few millimetres deep. Stand the candle in the water and light it. Place the glass over the top of the candle so its rim is standing in the water. Watch what happens as it burns up all the oxygen. (Water gets 'sucked' into the glass, making it look as if the candle is thirsty! What really happens is the air pressure gets lower as the oxygen is used up by the flame, so the liquid is drawn into the lower pressure space inside the glass.)

Talk about what it feels like to be really thirsty. Which charities/not-for-profits work to help people have safe drinking water? What do you think Jesus would think of them?

Celebration

Have a set of pictures – a lunchbox, a water bottle, a front door, a coat, a clock. Ask two leaders to be the goats and everyone else to be sheep. As each picture is shown, say:

Here's some _____. The goats say…

Leaders: 'Mine! Mine! Mine!'

But the sheep say…

All: 'Ours! Ours! Ours!'

Repeat for all the pictures (Here's some food… Here's some drink… Here's a welcome… Here's some clothing… Here's 24 hours in the day…).

Prayer

Jesus, help us to practise this really hard thing of sharing what we have with each other, so your world becomes a sharing place, not a grabbing place. Amen

Song suggestion

- 'When I needed a neighbour' – Sydney Bertram Carter

5

Serving

> After [Jesus] had washed their feet, had put on his robe, and had returned to the table, he said to them, 'Do you know what I have done to you? You call me Teacher and Lord – and you are right, for that is what I am. So if I, your Lord and Teacher, have washed your feet, you also ought to wash one another's feet. For I have set you an example, that you also should do as I have done to you. Very truly, I tell you, servants are not greater than their master, nor are messengers greater than the one who sent them. If you know these things, you are blessed if you do them.'
>
> JOHN 13:12–17

Activity: Fruit foot

You will need: fruit of different sorts, including grapes, small berries or raisins and slices of fruit like a cross section of a pear, apple, banana or pineapple; plates; pureed berries

Use the pureed berries as glue to stick pieces of fruit on to a plate to make a foot or footprint shape out of fruit. Eat the fruit foot before it goes brown.

Talk about Jesus washing his friends' feet: why did he do it? What did he have to give up to serve others in this way? The early church people gave up their money to serve others who were in need. Is there something we could give up to serve others?

Celebration

Who's the most important person you've ever met? Who's the most important person in this room? Who's the most important person in the world?

To his disciples, Jesus was the most important person in the universe! He had shown them he was not only a great leader but something even greater. His miracles and signs showed them he was God. The disciples were delighted to be his special friends: they had loved being cheered on with palm branches like the procession of a king the previous Sunday. And they looked forward to Jesus taking over the whole kingdom this very weekend. They were going to be princes and grand viziers and members of parliament and grand high governors and all the other wonderful powerful positions you get when you're friends with a king!

But in this story, Jesus got up, knotted the towel round his waist, poured water into the bowl, picked it up and knelt down. Then he washed his friends' feet one by one and dried them with the towel.

Nobody knew what to say. Jesus was the most important person in the room and there he was, doing the muckiest job.

'Do you understand what I have done for you?' he asked them. 'You call me "Teacher" and "Lord", and rightly so, for that is what I am. Now that I, your Lord and Teacher, have washed your feet, you also should wash one another's feet. I have set you an example that you should do as I have done for you' (John 13:12–15, NIV).

What an amazing man! What an amazing God! What amazing things does he want us to do to be like him? I don't think we need to actually wash anyone's feet, but what might they need us to do for them? Can you think of a way you can help someone else this week?

Prayer

Let's turn our story and our thoughts into a prayer.

Dear Jesus, you are the most important person on earth, but you chose to do the dirtiest job to serve others. Help us this week to serve other people and to be on the lookout for ways to make the world a better place. Let your kingdom come through us. Amen

Song suggestion

- 'O Jesus, I have promised' – John Ernest Bode

6

Biblical Teaching

Now on that same day two of them were going to a village called Emmaus, about seven miles from Jerusalem, and talking with each other about all these things that had happened. While they were talking and discussing, Jesus himself came near and went with them, but their eyes were kept from recognising him. And he said to them, 'What are you discussing with each other while you walk along?'...

They replied, 'The things about Jesus of Nazareth, who was a prophet mighty in deed and word before God and all the people, and how our chief priests and leaders handed him over to be condemned to death and crucified him. But we had hoped that he was the one to redeem Israel'...

Then he said to them, 'Oh, how foolish you are, and how slow of heart to believe all that the prophets have declared! Was it not necessary that the Messiah should suffer these things and then enter into his glory?' Then beginning with Moses and all the prophets, he interpreted to them the things about himself in all the scriptures.

LUKE 24:13–17, 19–21, 25–27 (abridged)

Activity: A lighthouse

You will need: the means to make a circuit; a light bulb; a battery

Enjoy creating circuits to light up the bulb. Talk about the way the power needs to flow around a complete circuit to light it up. The psalmist wrote that God's word is like 'a lamp to my feet' (Psalm 119:105). Jesus described himself as 'the light of the world' (John 8:12).

Talk about how Cleopas and his friend had some parts of the circuit, but needed Jesus to complete the circuit and make the light shine so they really understood

God's plan. We need to ask for Jesus' help when we find Bible stories we don't understand fully.

Celebration

Cleopas and his friend were feeling very down and were full of sad questions. They'd just seen their best friend Jesus killed on a cross, and they'd thought that everything they believed in was at an end. They thought they'd got it completely wrong and that Jesus was just a human being, not God at all. But then these rumours started up that people had actually seen Jesus alive again. Cleopas and his friend were feeling very down and full of sad questions. They decided to leave the city and walk home to Emmaus to get away from it all.

And as they walked along, feeling down and full of sad questions, someone came up beside them and asked them why they looked so down and sad. They told him what the matter was. But the stranger laughed and told them they were daft! 'Don't you see this had to happen?' he said. And as they walked along together, he explained to them what the scriptures said about God's big plan for the world and how it all came together in Jesus' dying and rising again. And as they walked along together, Cleopas and his friend started looking up and asking questions and laughing at the wonderful answers and seeing that everything they'd believed about Jesus was true and that it was even better than they'd thought!

As they got to their house, the stranger with so many answers and so many questions looked as if he was about to keep on walking, but Cleopas and his friend made him come in for a meal. As they sat down to eat, the stranger lifted up the bread to bless it, and suddenly Cleopas and his friend recognised that it wasn't a stranger at all; it was Jesus himself, alive and full of life and liveliness. But just as they recognised him, he disappeared. It was like a game of hide and seek! They were so full of excitement and questions and answers that they dropped everything and ran back to the city to find the other disciples. 'We've seen Jesus!' they shouted, all out of breath. 'So have we!' said the others. 'So have we!'

Cleopas and his friend knew scripture well, but they still didn't understand it all. They needed Jesus to come and help them see what it was all about.

Prayer

Invite two or three people to hide around the room and be ready to jump out of their hiding places when you raise your hands.

Jesus, sometimes trying to understand your plan for us is like being the seeker in a game of hide and seek. We search and search and search through the wonderful stories, poetry and laws in the Bible… and it takes so long… and we feel like giving up. And we try just one more time… and (*raise your hands*) there you are! Help us to keep seeking you in your wonderful world, in the wonderful people around us and in your wonderful word, the Bible. Amen

Song suggestion

● 'Tell out, my soul' – Timothy Dudley-Smith

7

Eating Together

> After this [Jesus] went out and saw a tax-collector named Levi, sitting at the tax booth; and he said to him, 'Follow me.' And he got up, left everything, and followed him.
>
> Then Levi gave a great banquet for him in his house; and there was a large crowd of tax-collectors and others sitting at the table with them. The Pharisees and their scribes were complaining to his disciples, saying, 'Why do you eat and drink with tax-collectors and sinners?' Jesus answered, 'Those who are well have no need of a physician, but those who are sick; I have come to call not the righteous but sinners to repentance.'
>
> LUKE 5:27–32

Activity: Table manners quiz

You will need: printouts of the quiz (download online); pens

Have fun with the quiz of table manners in different parts of the world.

Talk about what makes us feel safe when we sit down and eat with people we don't know very well. How safe would you feel sitting down to a meal with Jesus?

Celebration

Play the part of Levi's next-door neighbour.

It's absolutely shocking! That Jesus! They say he's the Son of God, but what does he do? He hangs out with the worst possible kind of person! I mean, would God want his Son to do that? I don't think so! God's Son would only spend time with good people. People who keep the rules. People like me, in fact!

I mean tonight – listen to that party going on next door! Music… dancing… bottles chinking… shouting and SO much laughter! Is that holy? I don't think so.

And do you know whose house it is? It belongs to Levi, one of the most criminal gangsters in town. He spends more time with the Romans than with his own people. He's a crook and a cheat and a materialistic money-grabbing swindler. But Jesus asked *him* to be one of his special friends! I mean! And because Levi was so happy to be picked out by the Son of God, he's gone and thrown a party for Jesus AND invited ALL his gangster friends. The street's been full of dodgy characters and their dodgy wives all night.

Perhaps Jesus is so daft he doesn't realise what sort of people they are? Perhaps – terrible thought – he actually LIKES being with people like Levi! Instead of with people like me, who always do the right thing and lead very good lives.

So I went next door to ask them to turn the music down a bit and said to him, 'Jesus, you want to watch yourself. You'll get a bad reputation if you sit down and eat with this sort of person. You should be in the synagogue being holy, not drinking and scoffing with these dreadful people. You don't belong here with them! Come and have a nice quiet sensible meal at my house and we can do some praying together.'

And he said to me, 'It's not healthy people that need a doctor, it's ill people. I haven't come to call people like you into a better life, but people like this.'

I don't know! Ridiculous! I mean, what sort of a God is this, who wants to give someone like Levi a second chance? I ask you! I wouldn't eat with Jesus – not in a million years. Would you?

Prayer

Thank you, Jesus, that you love to sit down with us, whether we're all sorted and good or whether we're a bit of a mess. Help us to enjoy spending time with you and with each other now. Amen

Song suggestion

- 'He's got the whole world in his hands' – traditional

8

Worship

> Now while Jesus was at Bethany in the house of Simon the leper, a woman came to him with an alabaster jar of very costly ointment, and she poured it on his head as he sat at the table. But when the disciples saw it, they were angry and said, 'Why this waste? For this ointment could have been sold for a large sum, and the money given to the poor.' But Jesus, aware of this, said to them, 'Why do you trouble the woman? She has performed a good service for me. For you always have the poor with you, but you will not always have me. By pouring this ointment on my body she has prepared me for burial. Truly I tell you, wherever this good news is proclaimed in the whole world, what she has done will be told in remembrance of her.'
>
> MATTHEW 26:6–13

Activity: Big kiss

You will need: a large cardboard X; old magazines or collage papers; scissors; glue (alternatively, you could use a papier mâché alphabet letter X box from craft stores)

Decorate the big kiss with the collage papers.

Talk about how the English word 'worship' comes from a word that means 'come close to kiss'. The woman in today's story loved Jesus so much she wanted to be close enough to kiss him. Do you find that surprising? Weird? Beautiful? Embarrassing? How did Jesus find it?

Celebration

As long as you don't have anyone who will be adversely affected by scents (they can affect people's breathing), pour out something very strongly scented and ask people to sit very still and put their hand up when they smell it. You might want to use an essential oil on an oil burner.

How interesting – some people smelled it almost straight away, some took longer and some never smelled it at all. The smell has spread around the room with no noise and is totally invisible. It's definitely there, but you can't see it or touch it.

In this story, some people were angry with the woma for wasting this very costly perfume on Jesus, when it could have been sold and the money given to the poor. But Jesus said, 'She has done a beautiful thing for me.'

We worship Jesus, too. How do we worship him? (*Songs, prayers, actions, service to others are just a few answers you might get.*) Some people never worship Jesus. Perhaps they've never thought of it or perhaps they think, like the people in the story, that it's a waste. It's like the perfume. But remember what Jesus thought of the woman who poured out the perfume. We bring our best to Jesus and hand it over to him, not because we're paying him or bribing him, but because we love him and want to show our love to him. We call this worship. To some people, it looks like a waste of time and effort. But to Jesus, it's something very beautiful.

Prayer

Have one full and one empty bowl on a table. Give everyone an empty cup. Say the water in the bowl is a symbol for what we want to offer Jesus in worship. Invite everyone to come and fill up their cup then pour it into the empty bowl. Explain that if they would like to offer the whole of themselves to Jesus, they could pour out the whole cup of water. If they're not sure they want to do that yet, they might pour out a little bit. If they would rather not pour any out, they could either drink it or put the cup of water on the table with the others. Nobody is watching how much they pour out: it's just between them and Jesus. Play a quiet song while this is happening.

Song suggestion

- 'Give me oil in my lamp' – traditional

9

Prayer

> [Jesus] was praying in a certain place, and after he had finished, one of his disciples said to him, 'Lord, teach us to pray, as John taught his disciples.' He said to them, 'When you pray, say: Father, hallowed be your name. Your kingdom come. Give us each day our daily bread. And forgive us our sins, for we ourselves forgive everyone indebted to us. And do not bring us to the time of trial.'
> LUKE 11:1–4

Activity: Calligraphy

You will need: calligraphy pens and inks; lined paper; alphabets to copy (find in books or online)

Give people a chance to draw the Lord's Prayer in calligraphy.

Talk about how sometimes taking longer to write something down and taking care over each letter can help us to relax and come more easily into God's presence. How might you prepare to meet God through mindfulness or meditation?

Celebration

Put a chair out in the middle of your gathering and declare that it's the 'Chair of Prayer'.

Today we've been thinking about one of the ways we grow closer to Jesus and that's by praying.

Invite someone to come and sit on the chair and share one thing they know about prayer. Repeat this a few times with different people and lots of applause.

Then invite someone (probably pre-arranged and from the team) to sit on the chair and share their favourite prayer and why they like it and when they say it.

Invite someone to share their bedtime prayer habit or what they pray before meals.

Invite someone (again, probably pre-arranged and from the team) to sit on the chair and share a time when they prayed and nothing seemed to happen but they kept on praying.

Repeat with someone who prayed and something changed more obviously.

We're trying to follow Jesus, so we want to do the things he and his friends did.

In today's story, Jesus prayed to God, and his disciples wanted to pray like he did. So Jesus taught them a special prayer, which Christians all over the world now pray. You don't have to be in a special place like the Chair of Prayer or in a church building to pray: you can pray anywhere at any time.

And it's much easier to talk about prayer than to get on and pray! So let's pray now…

Prayer

Pray the Lord's Prayer with actions (messychurch.org.uk/resource/lords-prayer-actions) or use the version from the end of *The Lord's Prayer Unplugged* (BRF, 2012).

Song suggestion

- 'What a friend we have in Jesus' – Joseph M. Scriven

10

Breaking Bread

Just after daybreak, Jesus stood on the beach; but the disciples did not know that it was Jesus. Jesus said to them, 'Children, you have no fish, have you?' They answered him, 'No.' He said to them, 'Cast the net to the right side of the boat, and you will find some.' So they cast it, and now they were not able to haul it in because there were so many fish. That disciple whom Jesus loved said to Peter, 'It is the Lord!' When Simon Peter heard that it was the Lord, he put on some clothes, for he was naked, and jumped into the lake. But the other disciples came in the boat, dragging the net full of fish, for they were not far from the land, only about a hundred yards off.

When they had gone ashore, they saw a charcoal fire there, with fish on it, and bread. Jesus said to them, 'Bring some of the fish that you have just caught.' So Simon Peter went aboard and hauled the net ashore, full of large fish, a hundred and fifty-three of them; and though there were so many, the net was not torn. Jesus said to them, 'Come and have breakfast.' Now none of the disciples dared to ask him, 'Who are you?' because they knew it was the Lord. Jesus came and took the bread and gave it to them, and did the same with the fish. This was now the third time that Jesus appeared to the disciples after he was raised from the dead.

JOHN 21:4–14

Activity: Breaking good

You will need: plates; pieces of different types of bread, such as sliced, pitta, poppadom and flatbread (alternatively, use pictures of bread and scissors)

Invite people to break the bread up and reassemble the pieces on the plate as something different. Then eat the resultant picture or sculpture (unless you've done the paper version).

Talk about how different the finished picture is from the original piece of bread. It's the same material but it's been transformed by your imagination and creativity. Breaking bread, either at a meal eaten together or at Communion, does something similar. A very ordinary, everyday object is transformed by God's creativity into something different. What changes do you see when people break bread together?

Celebration

It was just after Jesus rose from the dead and his friends were confused. Happy, but confused. They just weren't expecting Jesus to die or to come back from the dead, and it took a bit of getting used to. Everything was different. Everything had changed. It was exciting. But it wasn't comfy. So Peter and the others went out on the lake to do a bit of fishing. Fishing is nice and calming and normal if you're a fisherman.

But they fished all night and didn't catch anything!

When it got to morning and they were close to the shore again, someone called to them from the beach. 'Have you caught anything?' shouted a voice. 'No!' they all shouted back, rather grumpily. 'Throw your nets out on the other side of the boat!' shouted the voice. And when they did, straight away the nets filled up with over 100 fish! Peter remembered a time three years ago when something very much the same had happened in his boat, and he knew who the stranger on the beach was. He jumped into the water (yes – with all his clothes on!) and splashed his way to the beach, where the stranger was waiting. And yes! It was Jesus!

Jesus wasn't busy painting sunrises or creating galaxies that day. He was simply cooking bread for breakfast. So they brought some of the fish they had just caught as well and Jesus added them to the meal. Jesus broke the bread up and gave it, and the fish, to his friends, and they had the best picnic breakfast ever.

Breaking bread together is something we can all do, from the youngest person (well, maybe not a baby who just needs milk) to the oldest person, and from the person who doesn't know Jesus yet to the person who is already following him. When we break bread together at Communion or at our meal table, let's always remember Jesus is there with us, turning strangers into friends, putting the broken back together again in a new and unexpected way.

Prayer

Pass round a (gluten-free if necessary) bread roll and invite everyone to think about the way it's broken up between so many people. Now we all have a piece of the same bread inside us.

You might want to use one of the Messy Communion services from messychurch. org.uk/holy-communion.

Song suggestion

- 'As we are gathered, Jesus is here' – Authentic Publishing

11

Fellowship

[Jesus said,] 'I am the vine, you are the branches. Those who abide in me and I in them bear much fruit, because apart from me you can do nothing. Whoever does not abide in me is thrown away like a branch and withers; such branches are gathered, thrown into the fire, and burned. If you abide in me, and my words abide in you, ask for whatever you wish, and it will be done for you. My Father is glorified by this, that you bear much fruit and become my disciples. As the Father has loved me, so I have loved you; abide in my love. If you keep my commandments, you will abide in my love, just as I have kept my Father's commandments and abide in his love. I have said these things to you so that my joy may be in you, and that your joy may be complete.'

JOHN 15:5–11

Activity: Paper quilt

You will need: strips of patterned paper about 2 cm wide; scissors; glue; backing paper; print-offs of 'log cabin quilt' designs

Invite people to create their own paper log cabin quilt design by cutting paper strips to the right length and gluing them together carefully.

Talk about how quilts join up lots of scraps of fabric that otherwise would have been thrown away. How is that like the church? How do we make strong connections between us and God at the centre and between each other?

Celebration

Seat everyone in a circle, facing inwards. In the centre of the circle, have a box with spools of wool in it, ready to be unrolled.

Jesus had a big job for his disciples to do: he wanted them to change the whole planet! He wanted them to bring his kingdom of life-changing things like love, joy, peace, patience and much, much more to every part of the world. It was a huge job!

The disciples were great people. But Jesus knew that if they stayed close to him, they would be even greater, and that if they stayed in fellowship with each other, they would be greater still. And much more of the world would be changed for the better.

So before he died on the cross, he told them this:

(*Have somebody read the passage slowly and, as each sentence is read, unroll a spool of wool and pass the end to someone in the circle. Gesture to them to keep holding the end but to unroll some more wool and give it to someone else in the circle. They do the same, and at the same time, you can start another spool of wool unrolling in another part of the circle, as many as you need to, with everyone ending up holding on to the wool. Read the passage through several times if you need more time to get everyone joined in.*)

I am the true vine, and my Father is the gardener.
Remain in me, as I also remain in you. No branch can bear fruit by itself; it must remain in the vine. Neither can you bear fruit unless you remain in me.
I am the vine; you are the branches. If you remain in me and I in you, you will bear much fruit.
If you do not remain in me, you are like a branch that is thrown away and withers.
If you remain in me and my words remain in you, ask whatever you wish, and it will be done for you.
You did not choose me, but I chose you and appointed you so that you might go and bear fruit – fruit that will last. This is my command: love each other.
From JOHN 15

Look at us! We're all joined to each other and we're all joined to the centre. Jesus knows we need each other to do his work in changing the world, and we need to be connected to him.

But here's a challenge: we're all facing inwards! And if we want to change the world, we need to be looking outwards too! I wonder if we can carefully turn and face outwards without anybody dropping the vine… Let's pray while we hold the vine.

Prayer

Loving Jesus, thank you for the community around us. Help us to stay close to you and close to each other. Help us know we are never alone, however hard our different journeys may be. Amen

Now I wonder if we can untangle this wool together!

Song suggestion

- 'Make me a channel of your peace' – traditional

Get Messy! is a four-monthly subscription resource for Messy Church leaders. Each issue contains four session outlines (one per month), including planning sheets and take-home handouts, together with information on the latest resources and events. It also seeks to encourage and refresh Messy Church leaders by providing monthly Bible studies, stories from other Messy Churches, a youth column and a problem page.

Get Messy!
Session material, news, stories and inspiration for the Messy Church community

£4.60 per issue

brfonline.org.uk/collections/get-messy

INTRODUCTORY GUIDE

HOLYHABITS

MISSIONAL DISCIPLESHIP RESOURCES FOR CHURCHES

BIBLICAL TEACHING

They devoted themselves to the apostles' teaching and to fellowship, to the breaking of bread and to prayer.

HOLYHABITS

MISSIONAL DISCIPLESHIP RESOURCES FOR CHURCHES

FELLOWSHIP

They devoted themselves to the apostles' teaching and **fellowship**, to the breaking of bread and to prayer.

HOLYHABITS

MISSIONAL DISCIPLESHIP RESOURCES FOR CHURCHES

BREAKING BREAD

They devoted themselves to the apostles' teaching and fellowship, **to the breaking of bread** and to prayer.

HOLYHABITS

MISSIONAL DISCIPLESHIP RESOURCES FOR CHURCHES

PRAYER

They devoted themselves to the apostles' teaching and to fellowship, to the breaking of bread and **to prayer.**

HOLYHABITS

MISSIONAL DISCIPLESHIP RESOURCES FOR CHURCHES

SHARING RESOURCES

All the believers were together and had everything in common.

HOLYHABITS

MISSIONAL DISCIPLESHIP RESOURCES FOR CHURCHES

SERVING

All the believers were together and had everything in common, they sold property and possessions to give to anyone who had need.

HOLYHABITS

MISSIONAL DISCIPLESHIP RESOURCES FOR CHURCHES

EATING TOGETHER

They broke bread in their homes and **ate together** with glad and sincere hearts, praising God and enjoying the favour of all the people.

HOLYHABITS

MISSIONAL DISCIPLESHIP RESOURCES FOR CHURCHES

GLADNESS AND GENEROSITY

They broke bread in their homes and ate together **with glad and sincere hearts**, praising God and enjoying the favour of all the people.

HOLYHABITS

MISSIONAL DISCIPLESHIP RESOURCES FOR CHURCHES

WORSHIP

They broke bread in their homes and ate together with glad and sincere hearts, **praising God** and enjoying the favour of all the people.

HOLYHABITS

MISSIONAL DISCIPLESHIP RESOURCES FOR CHURCHES

MAKING MORE DISCIPLES

And the Lord added to their number daily those who were being saved.

HOLYHABITS

MISSIONAL DISCIPLESHIP RESOURCES FOR CHURCHES

Holy Habits is a way of life for those exploring or already actively living out the call of Jesus to 'follow me'. These resources are designed to help churches explore the habits creatively in a range of contexts. They provide ideas for worship services, groups and children's and family work along with practical suggestions to become involved in local community activities and projects.

Holy Habits
Missional discipleship resources for churches
Edited by Andrew Roberts
£4.99 each (discounts available for bulk purchases)

brfonline.org.uk/holy-habits

Enabling all ages to grow in faith

Anna Chaplaincy

Barnabas in Schools

Holy Habits

Living Faith

Messy Church

Parenting for Faith

The Bible Reading Fellowship (BRF) is a Christian charity that resources individuals and churches and provides a professional education service to primary schools.

Our vision is to enable people of all ages to grow in faith and understanding of the Bible and to see more people equipped to exercise their gifts in leadership and ministry.

To find out more about our ministries and programmes, visit

brf.org.uk